The CENTER FOR URBAN EDUCATION is an independent nonprofit corporation founded in 1965 under an absolute charter from the New York State Board of Regents. In June 1966, it was designated a regional educational laboratory under Title IV of the Elementary and Secondary Act of 1965. There currently are twenty regional laboratories throughout the country. The CENTER is in part a social research agency, in part an educative institution in the university tradition, in part an engineering laboratory where invented solutions to problems in urban educational form and policy are tested in cooperation with participating educators. The CENTER'S major goal is to clarify and improve education in the urban complexes of our pluralistic and democratic society.

Under the direction of its Communication Resources Committee, the CENTER publishes a wide variety of reports, monographs, books, and bibliographies, as well as two journals. A complete list can be found at the end of this publication. The aim of the material is to provide a basic source of useful and immediately relevant information.

# Politics and Reality in an American City

## The New Orleans School Crisis of 1960

by Morton Inger

━━━━━━━━━━━━━━━━━━━━━━━━━━━━━━━━━━━━━━

Morton Inger for the past several years has been a professional analyst of school desegregation and integration in cities throughout the United States. The present book evolved from his work in 1964-65 as a research assistant on a study conducted by the National Opinion Research Center. In 1966, he was assistant director of a study on school integration for the U.S. Commission on Civil Rights, and examined events in eight American cities. (This study is the basis of a forthcoming volume, co-authored with Robert T. Stout.) Since 1966, Mr. Inger has been a staff associate at the Center for Urban Education. He has degrees in law and political science, and has taught American history.

Portions of this book have also appeared in Robert L. Crain, *The Politics of School Desegregation* (Chicago: Aldine Publishing Company, 1968) ; copyright © 1968 by National Opinion Research Center.

*This publication was prepared pursuant to a contract with the United States Department of Health, Education, and Welfare, Office of Education, under the provisions of the Cooperative Research Program.*

*The research reported herein was supported by the Office of Education, Department of Health, Education, and Welfare, Project No. 5-0641-2-12-1.*

Additional copies as follows: 1–20, 25¢ each ; 21–50, 20¢ each ; over 50, 15¢ each. Payment *must* accompany order.

First printing: February 1969
Library of Congress Catalog Number: 69-15428

CENTER FOR URBAN EDUCATION
105 Madison Avenue, New York 10016
212–889–7277

# Acknowledgements

This work, though brief, has benefited from the assistance of many people. My primary debt is to Robert L. Crain, now of the Johns Hopkins University Department of Social Relations, who guided every step of the research, read and commented on early drafts, and provided the moral support which helped me carry through my end of the work. Grant McConnell and J. David Greenstone, of the University of Chicago Political Science Department, also read early drafts. Their critical suggestions and encouragement were invaluable to me. None of the above mentioned persons, however, has seen this final version, which contains new material and has undergone many changes since they last saw it. For the shape and organization of this final version, I am greatly indebted to Harris Dienstfrey for his careful editing and, beyond that, for the posing of questions that helped me clarify my thinking about New Orleans and politics. The responsibility for the content, of course, is mine.

I am also indebted to: Peter H. Rossi, of the Johns Hopkins University Department of Social Relations, who fathered the research and gave moral support to the man who supported me; Robert T. Stout, of the Claremont Graduate School, who conducted one-fourth of the interviews and wrote a perceptive and useful account of the New Orleans school crisis; G. William Foster, Jr., of the University of Wisconsin Law School, who generously loaned me his unpublished manuscript detailing the legal history of the New Orleans integration struggle; and Jane Tobier, whose careful proofreading has spared the reader many confusing moments.

This work would not have been possible without the cooperation of the many New Orleanians who granted interviews, explained the background, made their personal papers available, and served as continuing informants. To thank any of them by name, unfortunately, would be to expose them and betray the trust they gave me.

Although this work contains some criticism of the New Orleans school board, the criticism is not personal. I believe the careful reader will understand why President Kennedy once said that all Americans should be grateful to the New Orleans school board members.

*M. I.*

# TABLE OF CONTENTS

Politics must be understood through reason, yet it is not in reason that it finds its model. The principles of scientific reason are always simple, consistent, and abstract; the social world is always complicated, incongruous, and concrete. . . . Politics is an art and not a science, and what is required for its mastery is not the rationality of the engineer but the wisdom and the moral strength of the statesman. The social world, deaf to the appeal to reason pure and simple, yields only to that intricate combination of moral and material pressures which the art of the statesman creates and maintains.
—Hans J. Morgenthau, *Scientific Man vs. Power Politics*

## Introduction

This is a study of why one city, which seemingly was ready to be a leader in racial matters, became instead a center of resistance to school integration. When four Negro first graders entered two previously allwhite schools in New Orleans on November 14, 1960, the reaction by the city's extremists was so intense and went unchecked for so long that the city suffered a near catastrophe. Thousands of whites rampaged through the downtown business district hurling bricks and bottles. White children boycotted the two schools for a year, and for months an unruly crowd cursed, shoved, stoned, and spat upon the few white children who continued to attend one of the schools—while the nation watched on television.

The school board members who had desegregated the schools under federal court orders were ostracized by their friends and harassed and threatened in late night telephone calls. The state legislature removed the board members from office and tried to close the city's schools. Because the legislature also held up school funds and local banks refused to cash paychecks, many teachers and school personnel went unpaid for months. Downtown hotels and department stores reported their worst business slump since the Depression.

Critical as these events were, behind them lay the city's most serious problem—a lack of leadership. Consider New York City's school crisis of 1968—and then consider how much worse it could have been if: the mayor said that what happened in the schools was not his concern; the city's elite said the school issue was too controversial for them to get involved; the newspapers did not discuss the issue and the public in general acted as though nothing of importance was taking place; if, in short, the school board was left to handle the situation all by itself. This is what happened in New Orleans in the 1950s and in 1960.

Not one of New Orleans' leaders had even attempted to prepare the community for desegregation. As late as the fall of 1960—three years after Little Rock—they all believed that the New Orleans schools would never have to be desegregated. All of them were stunned when the federal judge handed down the order to desegregate. Even then, the leaders did nothing to prepare the community for a peaceful transition. Yet all this took place, not in some land-locked Bible-belt country town, but in the nation's second largest port, home of liberal French Catholicism and one of America's most cosmopolitan cities, thronged with tourists and businessmen from all over the world—cultured, civilized, heterogeneous New Orleans.

Though the situation in New Orleans justifiably arouses our moral indignation, this is not a muckraking book. Research into New Orleans revealed not an evil "power structure" conspiring in its clubs to "keep the niggers out of our schools," but a group of good men trying to hide from the obvious fact that their city would have to admit some Negro pupils to some of the white schools. The purpose of this book is to illuminate the conditions that permitted these men to avoid confronting this obvious fact.

The research of which this study of New Orleans is a part was conducted by a staff under the direction of Peter H. Rossi and Robert L. Crain at the National Opinion Research Center. The research consisted of an investigation into the politics of school desegregation in 15 large cities selected more or less at random.[1] The primary source of information for the study of New Orleans was a series of interviews of leading participants in the school desegregation controversy and other knowledgeable persons in New Orleans. These interviews were conducted by Robert T. Stout and the author in October 1964 and by the author in May 1965.

New Orleans was a unique case in two major ways: It was the only city in the sample that had experienced a campaign of organized violence in connection with school desegregation, and it was one of the only two Southern cities in the sample in which the elite—the influential bankers, attorneys, and businessmen—did not take part in the decisions that led to the desegregation of the schools. An isolated instance of violence tied to school desegregation occurred in Jacksonville, Florida, and, significantly, Jacksonville is the other city characterized by a withdrawal of the elite. In all the other cities, the elite took a public stand favoring a peaceful solution of the problem. In New Orleans these men refused to take a public stand even after violence had erupted. Eventually, they spoke out for a peaceful solution, but only after life in the city had been seriously disrupted by the continuing chaos and violence.

But the uniqueness of New Orleans had another turn to it. Like several other cities in the sample, New Orleans had had a successful reform movement. Reform began in 1946 with the election of deLesseps Morrison as mayor. Many of the people active in his campaign stayed in the reform fight and focused their efforts on the public schools. This movement (which still exists) exerted itself to "take the schools out of politics" and to elect "upright," civic-minded citizens to the school board. Both reforms succeeded: Morrison was still mayor in 1960, and the school board had been completely dominated by the reform candidates since 1952. New Orleans thus presented an unusual set of circumstances: a successful reform of the city and the schools, a withdrawal of the elite from the school desegregation issue, and then extensive chaos and violence when desegregation began.

The passivity of a reform mayor and an elite in the face of chaos, violence, and attempts by a governor and his legislature to close down a city's schools constitutes a major political failure—and a most puzzling one. For though most men wish to avoid unpleasant truths, the very nature of politics forces men in positions of leadership to be realistic and pragmatic—especially when their own interests are at stake. This did not happen in New Orleans. That it did not suggested that the cause was as basic as a flaw in the workings of the city's politics. As I will attempt to show, politics had in fact been pulverized in New Orleans by a series of developments and conditions dating back to the rise of Huey Long.

The story that follows necessarily revolves about "elites" and "power structures," so a matter of definitions is in order. Students of community power have been divided not only in their conceptions of the source of such power but also in their methods of examining it. Those researchers, usually sociologists, who use the "reputational" method tend to find a hierarchial, monolithic ruling elite in cities. According to this view, a "power structure" composed of the owners and top executives of the largest businesses in the community sets policy and plays the tune to which the understructure of lesser executives and the elected public officials dances. Those researchers, usually political scientists, who analyze specific issues tend to find, not a monolithic ruling elite, but a diverse, plural society with many points of influence and power. Such researchers have found that the men who exert influence vary from issue to issue, that the so-called "top" power holders "have so little in common and are so little in communication that consciously concerted action by them is all but impossible."*

* Martin Meyerson and Edward C. Banfield, *Politics, Planning, and the Public Interest* (Glencoe, Ill.: Free Press, 1955), p. 115. The statement I have quoted appears in a discussion of the results of research performed by Meyerson and Banfield in the city of Chicago. I want

Far apart as the two approaches and viewpoints are, the schism that separates them has been made wider by the ideological nature of the controversy. The adherents of the reputational school bear on their shoulders a heavy load of Marxian preconceptions about the power structure they have "discovered" —the men at the top are not only rich but are motivated solely by economic considerations; they constitute not only a conspiracy but one devoted to defeating the wishes of the democracy. The pluralist viewpoint is likewise grounded in ideology—the very *idea* of a power structure is so repugnant that it must be disproved. Consequently, much of the pluralists' writing has been devoted to denying that there are such animals as men of general influence.

In the hope of bringing some clarity into the study of community power, the research team which conducted the original investigations from which this more extended study is drawn decided to use both the reputational technique and the issue analysis. This dual approach not only provided verification of our findings but more importantly kept us from getting locked into a method that *presupposed* a given finding. When we examined the data, we found that New Orleans contained no "power structure"— as that phrase is commonly understood. But we did find men of general influence.

For want of a better term, I believe that the best way to refer to this group of general influentials is to call them the elite. In this study, that phrase shall be used to cover not only the men of general influence but also the strata from which these men are drawn.[2] Though the word "elite" has some unpleasant connotations of its own, I hope the use of this definition frees the term of its usual associations and makes it clear that I am not thinking of the New Orleans general influentials as the rulers of New Orleans.

Two more words or phrases need clarification at this point. "Desegregation" is clearly only a step toward the goal of true integration. But in 1960, especially in the South, "integration" meant little more than putting *a* Negro child in *a* previously allwhite school. Because quotes from the principal actors in the events covered by this discussion will use the word "integration" in this sense, I have stuck to the terminology then in use. In this discussion, then, "integration" and "desegregation" are synonyms for what we would call today the most token desegregation, that is, putting at least one Negro pupil into a previously allwhite school.

Finally, I wish to point out that the phrase "law and order" did not, in 1960, have the connotation of suppression of dissent that it has today.

---

to make clear that these authors do not go on to argue there is no such thing as a general influential, as I note is the tendency of many who hold the "pluralist viewpoint." Meyerson and Banfield were saying only that they found no such individuals in Chicago.

# Part One

## CHAPTER I

## The Destruction of Politics: Corruption and Reform

In the 1950s, even as late as the first part of 1959, New Orleans was expected to be a leader in peaceful desegregation in the South. Despite inequalities, whites and Negroes had lived in apparent harmony for decades, and New Orleans had perhaps less residential segregation than any large American city, North or South. In recent years, Negroes had been added to the police force, admitted to the public library, to all seats in the public buses, and to all the recreation facilities in the city; and all these changes had taken place smoothly and peacefully. An article in the *New Republic* in February 1959, was perhaps the first report to bring the surprising news that no leadership for peaceful school desegregation had yet emerged in New Orleans.

> There is no organized effort—as in Atlanta—to encourage people to think in advance of what the loss of the public schools would mean to them and to make their views known. . . . There is no organized defense of the schools by Protestant clergy or professional men and women, and most Negro leaders in New Orleans seem more interested in their personal political organizations than in matters of principle. The press—an anemic force in New Orleans life—gives its readers no hint that there is cause for concern about the future of the schools.[3]

Still, the article—and New Orleans moderates—saw hope for the city in what was termed the enlightened self-interest of the city's "power structure."

> Only the "power structure" of New Orleans business and finance appears to be beyond the reach of the WCC [White Citizens' Council]. They have no congregations or clients to consult or fear, and their main preoccupation is to keep New Orleans the flourishing center of a growing state. The forward-looking "reform" mayor,

deLesseps S. Morrison, whom they have kept in office for 13 years, looks coldly on anything that might sully the image of the modern progressive city he has helped create. The mayor, the chief of police, and the superintendent of schools are determined that there will be no mob rule in New Orleans. (The police have been professionalized under Mayor Morrison. . . .) And past experience indicates that coordination between city officials and the judiciary is such that they will succeed in keeping the peace—when and if desegregation of the schools is ordered.[4]

Clearly, much was expected of the Mayor—and the position of the article reflected the conviction of most observers of New Orleans in the 1950s. Judging from all outward appearances, the expectations were justified. "Chep" Morrison had been hailed by liberals as one of the new breed of Southern politicians concerned with attracting industry and shrugging off the old stereotype of the sleepy, prejudiced South. By quietly and gradually easing the harshness of the lives of New Orleans' large Negro population and simultaneously putting most of his effort into attracting more business to the city and consolidating the gains of the prosperous, conservative businessmen, Morrison built a base of power independent of both of Louisiana's major political factions. He closed down prostitution and gambling, put Negroes on the police force, and built up the city's port trade. "His city leadership," wrote political scientist Allan Sindler in 1956, "comprised a blend of practical politics, liberalism, good government, and aggressive leadership. . . ."[5] Morrison won the La Guardia Award for outstanding achievement in municipal affairs in 1953, and in 1957 *Fortune* named him as one of nine standout mayors and noted that he differed significantly from the traditional civic reformer in that he was not content simply to clean out City Hall but had also rejuvenated his city.[6] A progressive city—this was the image of New Orleans that Morrison's 13-year tenure had created. Most certainly, the Mayor and the business leaders would not permit anything to sully this image.

Yet in the fall of 1960, when the progressive image of New Orleans was indeed being sullied, the Mayor and the elite were sitting on their hands. Four months earlier, television station WDSU in New Orleans had editorialized: "It seems as if most community leaders are trying to look the other way. Few people want to talk about it. Newspapers play it down. . . . New Orleans is drifting in an atmosphere of unreality toward a catastrophe. . . ."[7] When the catastrophe arrived, neither Chep Morrison nor the elite would speak up in support of moderation.

To understand this response—or rather, the lack of it—it is necessary to refer to the developments that brought Morrison to the mayoralty. From the close of the nineteenth century until the mid-1920s, the State of Louisiana was governed by an alliance of urban upper classes and conservative planters. The discontent of the lower class whites was repressed by violence and smothered by their own desire to keep the Negro out of participation in politics. The challenge by the lower class whites finally came with Huey Long's assault on the conservative alliance in the 1920s. Long was elected governor in 1928 (after an unsuccessful attempt in 1924). Of the groups which opposed Long's challenge, the most powerful was the Choctaw Club of New Orleans, one of the few Southern party organizations that resembled the typical urban machine of the North and East. But, unlike the Northern machines, the Choctaws spoke for the most conservative business organizations of New Orleans. The Choctaws opposed, for example, Long's efforts to get natural gas at cheap rates for New Orleans residents, employer's liability laws, regulation of public utilities, and the federal income tax.

The intransigence of the Choctaws was intolerable to the Longs, and the Long faction, giving expression to the suppressed feelings of the rural lower class whites, ferociously attacked New Orleans and its factional machine. Unfortunately for New Orleans, the state constitution leaves Louisiana's cities vulnerable to interference by the governor and the legislature. To protect themselves, New Orleans' political leaders are always trying to forge an alliance with the governor; consequently, local affairs are aways being dragged into state politics. In 1930, Long formed his own New Orleans machine, the Louisiana Democratic Association, headed by Robert Maestri, who had saved Huey from impeachment in 1929. Though this organization worked *with* the Choctaws at first, by 1934 the alliance was over, and Huey Long was again declaring war on the Choctaws and the city administration.*

"War" is the correct word. In 1935, Longite Governor Oscar K. ("O.K.") Allen sent the National Guard into New Orleans and seized the offices of the city's registrar of voters. After getting the state candidates of the Long faction safely elected, the Guard retired from the city. The legislature then enacted laws designed to impair the fiscal solvency of New Orleans and bring the city to heel. City license fees were kept by the state, and New Orleans was prevented from borrowing in anticipation of its 1935 taxes. In 1935, the state took over supervisory control of the city's finances, and the city was pushed to the brink of bankruptcy.

In the winter of 1935-36, Longite Governor-elect Richard Leche let it be

---

* At this point, Huey was a United States Senator, but still very much in control of the Long faction and the statehouse.

known he would like to grant New Orleans the right to govern itself, but not if it would mean strengthening the hands of the Choctaws and the then mayor (T. Semmes Walmsley), whom the Choctaws had supported. In March 1936, Walmsley, taking the hint, announced that if he were the obstacle, he would resign, but only if local government would be restored to the city and the choice of his successor put to a vote of the people. Two days later, Governor Leche, Maestri, and the president of the New Orleans Dock Board (appointed by the governor) met in Hot Springs, Arkansas, to decide who should succeed Walmsley.

They chose Maestri. No Democrats dared (or wanted) to oppose him, and when the Republican candidate withdrew, the voting registrar declared Maestri to be the mayor (without the formality of an election) on August 17, 1936. In return for this favor, state aid was returned and a spurious form of self-government was entrusted to New Orleans. Control over local taxes, license fees, and city departments was quickly returned to the city and the Choctaws, but the legislature revamped the city's charter (without submitting the revisions to the electorate), giving Maestri almost absolute authority over the city government and patronage. The control was so extensive that Maestri took over the Choctaw organization. To complete the conquest of the city, Leche's legislature enacted a constitutional amendment *eliminating* New Orleans' mayoralty election for 1938, which meant that Maestri would not have to stand for election until 1942. The "enemy" now controlled the city.*

What were the business and other community leaders—the natural enemies of the Long faction—doing and saying while all this happened? The New Orleans *Times-Picayune,* home of conservatism in the state, put Walmsley's promise to resign on the front page, but had no editorial comment. The editorial cartoon for that day dealt with a proposal to build a memorial to the Battle of New Orleans and Old Hickory. The next day, the cartoon welcomed a surgeon's convention to the city. The day after Leche, Maestri, and the Dock Board president met in Arkansas to select the city's next mayor, there was still no editorial, and the cartoon showed a man and wife giving old clothes to the needy. At the end of June, Walmsley resigned, and the *Times-Picayune* praised his wise self-sacrifice, attacked the Choctaws (the traditional spokesmen for the conservative businessmen), and glowed over Leche's friendly gesture in promising to restore self-government to the city. There was no outcry or organized activity by the community's elite against the plunder of their city.

* For this brief summary of Louisiana political history, I have relied primarily on Allan P. Sindler, *ibid.*

Maestri ran a corrupt administration and kept a tight grip on the city—even to the point of turning out a majority vote for Earl Long when, in 1940, he campaigned against the city. Maestri's power sprang from three sources: exclusive control of patronage, support from the statewide Long faction, and a tie-in with New Orleans' organized gambling (run by Frank Costello of New York). The first source got out the vote, the second provided the supportive and protective legislation, and the third provided the muscle and the money.

Maestri was easily reelected in 1942, and in 1946 he was again considered a certain victor. But his ten years of corruption had angered many upper-middle-class people. In 1945, they cast about for a candidate and chose a professional politician named "Bathtub Joe" Fernandez; but six weeks before the primary, Fernandez announced he was supporting Maestri. The independents asked a dozen men to make the race, but all were afraid to do it. They then asked Colonel deLesseps Morrison, just back from the Army and still in his uniform, to run, and he agreed. The handsome Morrison, scion of a 150-year-old Creole family, was young (only 34), Catholic, had a good war record, and had served two years as an anti-Long state representative before the war. Though he had somewhat of a playboy reputation, that was no serious handicap in fun-loving New Orleans. Still, for all his many attractions, no one expected him to beat Maestri.

But a group of women worked so hard for Chep Morrison—with door-to-door canvassing and a famous march down Canal Street with brooms—that Morrison surprised everyone and upset Maestri. As Maestri said, "Them widow women beat me."[8] As it happened, very few of these women were widows; in fact, they quickly became known as the "Girls."

Morrison took office pledged to give New Orleans an honest reputation and to have his city outstrip Miami as the "gateway to Latin America." In his first year in office, he made three trips to Latin America and visited 20 countries; in his first six years, he made 12 such sales trips, opening up the equivalent of consular offices in Latin American countries. (He also drew some criticism for what many called his pleasure cruises away from his city.) Civic and business leaders formed a group called Greater New Orleans, Inc., and launched a campaign to attract industry to the city. Morrison and the businessmen worked well together and became friends. Though some efforts to attract industry had begun prior to Morrison's election (notably with the International House development, a club for shippers), the real impetus was provided by Morrison's dynamic salesmanship. In 1948, businessmen gave $100 thousand and the Pan-American Life Insurance Company loaned the city $750 thousand to build the Pan-American Mart, an attraction for the city's port users. In that year, New Orleans, whose port had ranked sixteenth in the country in dollar volume and exports after World War I, became the nation's second busiest port. The port was not the only part of the city's growth. In 1951, more than $200 million worth of new industry moved into the area, and in 1952, another $150 million moved in.

Morrison led the way for a multimillion dollar railroad consolidation program, the elimination of underpasses, and the construction of a $15 million railroad terminal. Boulevards were widened and some slums cleared out long before the federal urban renewal program began. On the cleared land, a $20 million civic center was put up.

Morrison lived up to the expectations of the reformers. A nonpartisan commission of civic leaders chosen by Morrison prepared and won for the city a new "home rule" charter which replaced the mayor-commission form of government with the mayor-council form. (But it did not provide much protection from state legislative control.) The charter contained provisions designed to achieve "efficiency" and "economy" and provided for two (out of seven) at-large members of the city council. Some of the "politics" was thus taken out of government.

Morrison's chief campaign support continued to come from the Girls, who, by the mid-50s, had an extensive ward organization. Morrison, of course, had developed his own political base by his deeds in office, and, unlike most reform mayors, he had formed his own political organization, the Crescent City Democratic Association. He was liked by the elite, the middle class reformers, and the Negroes, but disliked by the die-hard segregationists and the upstate rural Protestants. He was reelected in 1950, 1954, and again in 1958.

But New Orleans did not fulfill the early promise of economic wealth. By the late 1950s, though the port was still thriving and expanding, other areas of the economy were not. Some major companies were leaving the area, and New Orleans was once more getting the reputation as one of America's sleepier cities. Morrison had found city government too confining and was trying to become governor, and the businessmen showed signs of having lost interest in the rejuvenation of their city. The organization they had formed, Greater New Orleans, Inc., turned out to be just an advertising outfit and not a very effective one at that. International House, an institution thought to be one of the rejuvenating features of the mid-40s, turned out to be nothing more than a social institution for people with third-generation wealth. In 1958, 1959, and 1960, not one major company moved to the New Orleans area.

Furthermore, despite Morrison's long tenure and despite the zeal and organization of the Girls, reform never became institutionalized. Political power had not evolved to the "better element." Morrison had built an organization dependent on his personal leadership. The Girls, unable to interest influential men—most of whom are businessmen—to run for the school board, remained an autonomous political movement. When Morrison resigned office in 1961, the city council appointed a man who was not in Morrison's organization to succeed him, and the new mayor defeated the reformers' candidate in 1962.

In one area of the city's life, however, reform had become institutionalized. Encouraged by their success in electing Morrison in 1946, the Girls had turned their zeal to the public schools. The school board, which had become little more than a job disbursement agency for Maestri, had allowed an already weak school system to deteriorate. All jobs, from principals to janitors, were distributed as patronage. Patronage needs, for example, determined the number of maintenance workers to be hired. In 1948, there was one maintenance worker for every 439 students in the New Orleans schools. The ratio in other cities was: Philadelphia, one to 783; Cincinnati, one to 1255; Baltimore, one to 1760; and New York, one to 3950. And despite the huge maintenance force, many school buildings were in such a bad state of repair they were condemned by the state fire marshal, and an independent study in 1948 rated 33 per cent of the high schools, 37 per cent of the white elementary schools, and 84 per cent of the Negro elementary schools as "unfit for use."[9] As for such a substantive matter as the curriculum, the school board members, who conducted their meetings in private, were so busy deciding who should be added to the stenographic pool or the janitorial staff that they simply ignored it.

When the Girls decided to clean up the situation in the public schools, they did so in the classic terms of reform, by "taking the school board out of politics." In 1948, there was an opening on the school board, but the Girls could not find a man willing to run for it.* The elite said—as they had in the 1930s with the installation of the Long-dominated Maestri government, and as they were to say again in 1960 concerning the desegregation of the schools—that their businesses were too sensitive to allow them to take part in controversial issues. So one of the Girls—Mrs. Jacqueline Leonhard—made the race.

Jackie Leonhard was a maverick. In a city where one must be native-born to be accepted, she was from Oklahoma, and part Indian to boot. In a Catholic city, she was a divorcée. In the union-hating South, she was avowedly pro-

---

* The board is composed of five members serving staggered six-year terms. Every two years, the voters elect one or two members depending on whether terms of one or two expire at that time.

labor and apparently pro-Negro. Her liberalism made her an anomaly even among the Girls. Typical of reform groups, the Girls were and are more interested in the structure of government—eliminating corruption, instituting civil service, and finding "quality" candidates—than in the content of the government's policies. In terms of their specific views, the Girls represent a wide range of political opinions and include many, for example, who were for Goldwater in 1964. Moreover, despite their political vigor, New Orleans women do not ordinarily run for political office. It is considered unbecoming for a Southern lady.

Only an unorthodox woman would have done it in 1948. Mrs. Leonhard did and won. When, after she took office, the all-male school board tried to keep her out of its deliberations by retiring to the men's room, she threatened to follow the board, and that brought it back out. The reform of the school system had begun.

Two years later, the Girls were able, finally, to persuade two men to run for the board, an administrator at Tulane University, Dr. Clarence Scheps, and a young engineer named Paul Besse. The Girls estimate that they made 60,000 phone calls in the campaign for these two men. Both were elected, and, with a three-to-two majority, the reformers immediately elected Mrs. Leonhard president of the board. Two years later, in 1952, they captured the remaining two seats by running Theodore Shepard, a shrimp importer, and Emile Wagner, an attorney and bank official. The campaign for these two men stressed that they were young and "independent." Sweeping the board, the reformers lowered the average age of the school board members by over twenty years.

The next several years brought a few changes of detail. By 1954, the reform movement had "gone respectable." Since Mrs. Leonhard's unorthodoxy was no longer needed, she was considered by many reformers to be unacceptable. She was defeated by Matthew Sutherland, an insurance company executive who was supported by many of the Girls. In 1956, Scheps and Besse stepped down, and the Girls recruited and elected Louis Riecke, a well-known lumber company executive who had worked hard in Chep Morrison's campaigns, and Lloyd Rittiner, an employee of an oil company. It was these five—Ted Shepard, Emile Wagner, Matt Sutherland, Louis Riecke, and Lloyd Rittiner—young, honest, civic-minded, nonpolitical businessmen or professionals, but none of them members of the community's elite, who constituted the school board during the desegregation crisis of 1960.

The reform movement had succeeded in taking the school board out of politics, but now there was a political decision to be made.

## CHAPTER II

# Crisis And Silence

### 1952-1960: THE WASTED YEARS

The series of events that rocked New Orleans in 1959 and 1960 were set in motion by the filing of a suit by the NAACP against the Orleans Parish* school board in September 1952. The suit was filed in the name of several Negro parents. At first the case lay dormant while the local NAACP awaited a signal from the national office. The signal did not come for four years—until after the final decision by the U.S. Supreme Court in the school segregation cases.[10] And then a lengthy process began.

Of the many court decisions in the case (known as *Bush v. Orleans Parish School Board*), the first was delivered on February 15, 1956, by Judge J. Skelly Wright of the federal District Court in New Orleans. Among other things, his decision enjoined the Orleans school board from requiring and permitting racial segregation and directed the board to "make arrangements for admission of children . . . on a racially nondiscriminatory basis with all deliberate speed . . ."[11]

The school board, composed entirely of the reform candidates, made no such arrangements. It was determined to use "every legal and honorable means" of maintaining segregation. When asked if the board was planning for eventual integration just in case the Supreme Court upheld the District Court's decree, Dr. Clarence Scheps, Tulane University's comptroller (and one of the first men elected to the board by the reform movement), said, "Absolutely not. We will not integrate. We couldn't integrate even if we wanted to."[12]

---

* In Louisiana, the parish is the area known as the county in most other American states. Geographically, Orleans Parish and the city of New Orleans are identical; historically, the two units developed with different political functions, and though the two were consolidated in 1870, some functions are still distinct. The school board is a parish board responsible directly to the state, not to the city.

Judge Wright seemed determined to enforce his decision, and the school board appeared equally determined to fight the case. The board's attorney, Sam Rosenberg, a local leader of the Anti-Defamation League, told the board the law was against it and asked to be relieved of the task of arguing the case. The board retained Rosenberg as its general counsel but hired a former assistant attorney general for the state, Gerard Rault, to handle the desegregation case.* Rault was the attorney for a downtown savings and loan association of which school board member Emile Wagner, one of the city's leading segregationists, was the president. Rault and Wagner were also close personal friends.

For the next three years, from 1956 to 1959, the school board resisted the integration decision of Judge Wright, appealing his rulings through the federal court system. If nothing else, the appeals had the advantage (from the school board's point of view) of delaying desegregation by keeping the case in the courts. The United States Court of Appeals and the United States Supreme Court affirmed the decisions of the District Court.[13]

Throughout this period, the board made no efforts, either publicly or behind the scenes, to prepare itself, the city, or the school staff for integration. Nor was any member of the city government engaged in any such preparation. When asked (in 1964) about the lack of preparations, the board members explained that preparations were considered unnecessary because they had firmly believed, as Dr. Scheps had said in 1956, that the New Orleans schools were never going to be integrated.**

Finally, in 1959, the Negro plaintiffs, silent throughout this period, urged further orders by the court. Accordingly, on July 15, 1959, more than three years after he had directed the board to begin making arrangements, Judge Wright ordered it to file a desegregation plan by March 1, 1960.[14] Judge Wright, a native New Orleanian and a close friend of many of the principal actors in this drama, including Mayor Morrison, Sam Rosenberg, Emile Wagner, and Gerard Rault, later changed this date to May 16, 1960, at the request of the school board.

Mayor Morrison said nothing publicly. Privately, he indicated he would have nothing to do with the school controversy. He had run for governor in 1956 and 1960 and wanted to run again in 1964. To win, he needed the votes of many segregationists. He was not going to ruin his chances by being identi-

* Part of Rault's salary was paid by the state.

** Unless otherwise indicated, all quotations and paraphrases herein are based on personal interviews conducted by the author or by Robert T. Stout.

fied with the federal government's attempt to put Negro children in the white schools of New Orleans.

The extra time allotted by Judge Wright was used by the board to conduct a poll of the parents. The president of the board, Lloyd Rittiner, believed that if it could be shown that a majority of parents would rather have token integration than have no schools at all—and he was certain this could be shown—it would be easier to draw Mayor Morrison into support of the board. On April 22, the school board sent a letter to the parent or guardian of every pupil in the public schools asking him to check his preference between the following alternatives.

1. I would like to see the schools kept open even though a small amount of integration is necessary.
2. I would like to see the schools closed rather than be integrated even in small amounts.

The emphasis on the small amount of integration and the use of the phrase "I would *like to see*" were apparently attempts to load the questions in favor of alternative number one. But to everyone's astonishment, almost 82 per cent of the white parents voted to close the schools. The size and speed of the response was just as impressive—within two weeks of the mailing, almost 64 per cent of the white parents responded. (See Appendix I for tabulation.) The results were announced on May 8, just seven days before the board was to come up with a desegregation plan. Rittiner, who prior to the tabulation had said that the poll would "wake up the people to the problem they face," was so stunned by the results that he now said he would disregard the Negroes' ballots (which were overwhelmingly in favor of keeping the schools open) and "abide by the wishes of the white people because they are the people who support the school system and elect us to the school board."[15]

On May 16 the board told the court that it had no desegregation plan. Judge Wright responded by supplying his own plan ordering the desegregation of all first grades at the opening of school in September.[16] Though great attention had been directed to school desegregation in many cities, particularly in Little Rock, and though the city had been on notice for ten months that it had to come up with a desegregation plan, board members and civic leaders, as they later told an interviewer, were "stunned" by this order. One reason they perhaps legitimately were "stunned" was the milieu of the city, for, one by one, all of the community's institutions had either taken a stand opposing integration or else had retreated and maintained a frightened silence.

## THE GUBERNATORIAL ELECTIONS OF 1959 AND 1960

The hostility of the governor, the state superintendent of education, and the state legislature to any position short of die-hard segregation became clear during the gubernatorial elections in December 1959 and January 1960. Ever since the rise of Huey Long in 1928, Louisiana state political campaigns, though one-party in name, had been fought out along stable bifactional lines, and though Huey Long was looked upon as a hero by the Negroes, neither faction's support was based on the promulgation of any racial ideas, and the state's elections did not hinge on racial questions. The well-organized Long faction ran on an agrarian welfare-state program; the more amorphous anti-Long faction was a loose alliance of urban upper classes and rural planters who campaigned for "good government" and "sound administration," i.e., a favorable atmosphere for business and economy in government.

But the results of the first primary election in December 1959, forced the issue of racial segregation into prominence. State Senator Willie Rainach, one of 11 candidates for governor, discarded his attachment to Longist programs and campaigned as an out-and-out racist, branding all the other candidates "soft" on segregation. (School board member Wagner campaigned actively for Rainach.) Rainach was eliminated in the primary, but he drew such a big vote that he remained a key factor in the run-off between Chep Morrison and Jimmie Davis, the hill-billy singer and composer of "You Are My Sunshine."

As the table indicates, to win the run-off, Davis or Morrison would need the support of Rainach and his followers.

FIRST PRIMARY FOR GOVERNOR OF LOUISIANA, DECEMBER 5, 1959

| Candidate | Vote | Percentage |
| --- | --- | --- |
| Morrison | 278,956 | 33.1 |
| Davis | 213,551 | 25.3 |
| Rainach | 143,095 | 17.0 |
| James Noe | 97,654 | 11.6 |
| William Dodd | 85,436 | 10.1 |
| Six others | 23,917 | 2.9 |

Source: *PAR Analysis* No. 84, Public Affairs Research Council of Louisiana, Inc., January 1960.

The run-off was the first since Huey Long's election in 1928 that involved no representative of the Long faction. The principal Long candidate, James Noe, had finished fourth. Furthermore, neither survivor of the first primary was a strong anti-Longite. Davis always appealed for cross-factional support. He had sung his way to a previous term as governor (1944-1948) on an apolitical campaign of "peace and harmony," and his motto was: "I Never Done Nobody No Harm."[17] Morrison was a loner who, despite his connection with the "good government" movement and thus anti-Longism, had built his own base of support in New Orleans independent of either faction. Though both men were "in" the anti-Long faction, neither one could be called the candidate "of" the anti-Long faction.

Thus, the relatively stable bifactionalism of the preceding 30 years was obliterated in this campaign. In its place was substituted a contest over who could best preserve segregation. Davis abandoned his peace and harmony theme and went about the state reminding the voters that all the Negro precincts in New Orleans had given Morrison a huge majority in the primary. The moderates in New Orleans—Morrison's personal friends—were treated to the disheartening spectacle of their good-government, reform mayor stumping the state for the votes of the segregationists while his city's school board was under court orders to come up with a desegregation plan. Morrison recounted his "vigorous positive actions to maintain segregation"[18] and reminded the voters that Davis had never taken a stand on this issue prior to the run-off and had operated an integrated honky-tonk in California. But Morrison's appeal for segregationist support was hopeless; deservedly or not, he had the reputation of a racial progressive. Davis won, polling 54.1 per cent of the vote.

Governor Davis, his attorney general, the state commissioner of education, and the state legislators seemed determined to preserve segregation even if the only way was to close the New Orleans schools. Previous state administrations had passed laws requiring segregation in the schools, authorizing the closing of desegregated schools, and providing for the removal of school employees who aided desegregation. The current administration was prepared to utilize all such legislation—and it added some new legislation of its own.

It passed laws prohibiting the granting of school funds to desegregated schools, gave the governor the right to close *all* the schools in the state if any one were integrated and to close any school threatened with violence or disorder. The most subtle was one reserving to the legislature the exclusive right to integrate the schools, the legislature's sham gesture toward meeting the requirements of the *Brown* decision. A corollary to this act was one which provided that where a school board was under court order to desegregate, the governor would supersede the board and run the schools until the legislature desegregated them.

Armed with these statutes, Louisiana's Attorney General, Jack P. F. Gremillion, went into the state courts to block the federal desegregation order. In March 1960, in response to one of the suits filed by Gremillion, the Louisiana Court of Appeals ruled that the Orleans Parish school board no longer had power to "classify" (as white or Negro) its schools.[19] When the school board told Judge Wright on May 16 that it had no plan, it was relying on this state court decision as having prevented it from producing a plan.

## THE CATHOLIC CHURCH AND THE PAROCHIAL SCHOOLS

New Orleans, with approximately two-thirds of its population Catholic, has by far the largest Catholic diocese in the South; in 1960, half the total number of Catholics in the entire South lived in the Archdiocese of New Orleans. Largely because of the statements and actions of its Archbishop, Joseph Francis Rummel, the diocese had the reputation of being liberal on race relations, and, at one point, the hierarchy seemed to be paving the way for community acceptance of desegregation. As early as 1949, Rummel had cancelled a Holy Hour service because the religious procession would be segregated. That same year, he had ordered the "white" and "colored" signs removed from pews in the churches. In a pastoral letter in 1953 he had written, "Let there be no further discrimination or segregation in the pews, at the Communion rail, at the confessional and in parish meetings, just as there will be no segregation in the kingdom of heaven. . . ."[20] On the Sunday following Judge Wright's February 15, 1956 ruling that the Orleans Parish public schools would have to be integrated, Archbishop Rummel proclaimed in a pastoral letter that racial segregation was "morally wrong and sinful because it is a denial of the unity and solidarity of the human race as conceived by God in the creation of man in Adam and Eve."[21]

New Orleans' Catholics had suffered Rummel's earlier moves in silence, but this step seemed to be too much for them to bear. Some priests refused to read the pastoral letter, and, that night, a cross was burned on the lawn of Rummel's residence. Several legislators, some of them Catholic, threatened to give the state police power to keep the parochial schools segregated.

Five months later, Rummel tried to put his theology into practice and learned how profoundly opposed to it his parishioners were. He announced that racial integration of the parochial schools on a grade-a-year basis would begin in September 1957. The reaction from his parishioners was swift and overwhelming. They picketed his rectory, and, led by school board member Emile Wagner, they appealed directly to Pope Pius XII to overrule Rummel's pronouncement on segregation. A "high Church authority" in the Vatican newspaper sternly rebuked the petitioners for their "doctrinal error" and "breach of discipline" and reminded them that, in October 1955, the Vatican newspaper had commended the Archbishop of New Orleans for his stand against segregation.

Despite the encouragement from above, the pressures from below proved too much. Contributions to the church declined seriously, and pledges for capital projects were not honored. In September 1957, the date set for the beginning of racial integration of the parochial schools, the Archbishop was silent and the parochial schools remained segregated. In fact, from July 31, 1956, until the first week of July 1959, Rummel made no further public statements on the subject. According to one unverified account, Rummel's long silence was in part due to his having been persuaded by his advisors that his pronouncement had gone beyond the demands of the Negroes. His advisors are said to have pointed to the silence of the Negro community in New Orleans and to the lack of initiative by the Negro attorneys in the *Bush* case.

Finally, in July of 1959, Rummel, still retreating but trying to find some place to draw the line, lamely announced that the parochial schools would be integrated "at the earliest possible opportunity and definitely not later than when the public schools are integrated"; but when the date for public school desegregation arrived, the parochial schools had once again withdrawn their own desegregation plans. Though Rummel, had, in 1956, threatened excommunication for any Catholic legislators who either worked for or voted for laws which would force segregation on parochial schools, the state legislature, in late summer of 1960, threatened to withdraw the tax-exempt status of church property and to cut off funds the state was providing the parochial schools for buses and textbooks.

In 1959, Monsignor Henry C. Bezou, superintendent of the New Orleans parochial school system, had said, "segregation in the parochial schools can be ended with the stroke of a pen. The Archbishop of San Antonio did it (in 1954). . . . And it will happen here."[22] Bishop Vincent Waters of Raleigh, North Carolina did it, too, in 1954, *prior* to the Supreme Court decision and despite virulent protests.* And in the Upper South, as early as 1947, St.

---

* Neither Raleigh nor San Antonio has as large a parochial school system as New Orleans. Raleigh has few Catholics; San Antonio a substantial number.

Louis's Archbishop Ritter desegregated his schools and warned he would excommunicate any who opposed the step. Ritter's move preceded by seven years the integration of St. Louis's public schools. Bishop Waters showed that it could be done if the hierarchy was willing to fight it out. But Rummel, a gentle, tired old man, seemed not to have the strength.* The collapse of leadership from the church greatly undermined the already isolated school board.

## MODERATES AND LIBERALS

By 1960, eight years had elapsed since the initial filing of the suit by the Negro parents, four years since Judge Wright directed the school board to begin making arrangements for desegregation, and nine months since Judge Wright had ordered the board to file a plan. Yet, in early 1960, not one white moderate group in New Orleans was publicly supporting school desegregation. The Girls were quiet as well. Such a situation was by no means typical of the South. In Atlanta, for example, a housewives organization (HOPE) was publicly working for acceptance of desegregation long *before* the Atlanta school board was ordered to desegregate.

After 1954, a few New Orleans groups had tried but had failed to promote even discussion of the issues. In 1958, a rabbi of a well-to-do congregation had organized an interfaith group of clergy to study race relations, but Jews were "suspect" on the issue, and the group quickly collapsed. Prominent Jewish leaders learned to keep discretely in the background of "moderate" efforts. The Catholic hierarchy backed the efforts of another such organization, but because of the pronouncements by Archbishop Rummel, this group, too, was suspected of being integrationist, and the organization collapsed.

Another serious obstacle to "moderate" activity was the charge that desegregation efforts were "communistic." In 1955, the Southern Conference Educational Fund, an antisegregation organization with headquarters in New Orleans, found a hundred sponsors for a forum on school integration. Mayor Morrison agreed to proclaim December 10 to 15, 1955, "Human Rights Week," and the school board granted permission for use of a school auditorium. But on December 10, the Young Men's Business Club passed a resolution urging a boycott of the forum because someone had charged that a leader of SCEF was linked to Communism. The school board rescinded its

---

* On October 9, 1960, Rummel, 83 years old, fell and broke an arm and a leg. The men acting in his absence had no desire for a fight against the segregationists. The parochial schools were not integrated until 1962, two years *after* the public schools had paved the way.

permission for use of the auditorium, and the Mayor refused to proclaim Human Rights Week. When the respectability of the sponsors—mainly social workers and professors—was pointed out, the school board offered to let the *sponsors* hold the meeting if they dissociated themselves from SCEF. The sponsors accepted this condition, but the school board stalled, forced a postponement, and finally yielded. When the forum was held on December 15, it marked the first sympathetic public hearing of the integration issue in New Orleans. Nevertheless, the Communist charge discouraged attendance at future forums, and the sponsors eventually abandoned the effort.

Another group, Save Our Schools, Inc. (SOS), organized in 1959, but kept itself hidden until the announcement of the school board's postcard poll in April of 1960. Composed of social workers, Tulane professors and their wives, and some lawyers and businessmen, SOS had a high percentage of Jews, pro-integration Catholics, and non-Southerners. None of its members was in the elite. The organization was immediately stigmatized as "radical" and "integrationist" because it was made up of the same people who had been active in the earlier efforts to promote favorable discussions of integration. These were New Orleans' liberals. So great was this stigma that the group was totally unable to attract the moderates of the city even though SOS strategy emphasized open rather than integrated schools.

At the same time, while the voices of moderation were silent, the voices of die-hard segregationism were plainly heard. The White Citizens' Council held mass rallies, and an endless stream of obscene, threatening phone calls poured in on the board members and other moderates throughout each night.

## THE ELITE

Throughout this period, the elite remained silent. They were "out" to anyone who wanted to talk to them about the schools. Their position can be seen in the editorials of the *Times-Picayune,* which described the city's dilemma in an editorial on June 26, 1960, something over a month after Judge Wright had ordered integration of the school system's first grade.

> Public education, unquestionably, is a foundation of democracy, but whether public education can survive the forced integration of schools in a community like ours, with a large Negro population and ingrained customs, remains to be seen. Forced integration . . . is a tragedy; just as closing of the schools would be a tragedy.

Faced with this choice, the *Times-Picayune* refused to take a stand.

The choice as to whether closed schools are to be preferred to integrated schools is one which the people themselves must make. We would not presume to make it for them.[23]

Through its postcard poll, the board already knew the choice the white people would make—close the schools.

## THE SCHOOL BOARD'S DILEMMA

This was the atmosphere and the environment within which the four moderate segregationists on the school board were forced to operate. New Orleans, unique among Southern cities for the heterogeneity of its white population— Germans, Irish, Italians, French, Spanish, Middle-Europeans, Catholics, and Protestants—was speaking with one voice: the voice of resistance to and defiance of the federal courts. Viewed in this context, the board's report to Judge Wright in May 1960 that it had no plan for desegregating the schools can be seen as a moderate position stopping short of a refusal to come up with a plan. It was an admission of helplessness and a call for help. Help came from Judge Wright. By providing the plan himself, he relieved the board of the onus of having taken any initiative toward integration.

Nevertheless, help would also have to come from the community. The schools, after all, are a community institution. Endorsement by the liberals in SOS was not enough. If the schools were to be kept open, in all likelihood the mayor or the elite would have to take a stand. But even if they remained silent and passive, it was possible that a statement from a group of respectable nonliberals might save the schools. On June 1, the citywide PTA passed an innocuous resolution in support of keeping the schools open, but a week later, at a meeting which drew a great deal of advance publicity, the open schools resolution was voided and all school PTAs that persisted in support of the resolution were threatened with expulsion.

The five school board members were thus faced with the requirements of federal laws and courts on the one hand and the determination of all the branches of the state government to prevent the implementation of this law on the other hand. For one board member, Emile Wagner, the choice was clear—to continue working against Judge Wright's order. (Wagner, an organizer of the New Orleans White Citizens' Council, drafted some of the laws by which the legislature later tried to take over control of the New Orleans school board.) But for the other members of the school board, the issue was not so clear. These four men—Matthew Sutherland, Louis Riecke, Theodore Shepard, and Lloyd Rittiner, the president of the board—believed in segregation, and Rittiner had briefly been a member of a White Citizens' Council.

But these were not Southern "crackers," filled with hate; these were respectable businessmen who wanted to do what was "right." Indeed, they—and Wagner, too—had been recruited by the reform movement because of their respectability and their interest in and commitment to the public schools. Yet to do what was "right" meant to go against intensely held local customs, customs to which the men themselves subscribed. These four men faced a severe personal conflict, and they faced it alone.

Having been removed from politics, the school board had to make a political decision, and had to make it without the support of any major institution in the city. Isolation made the four moderate board members desperate. Two of them considered resigning. The board's mood came to public attention on June 20, 1960, when the board passed a resolution asking Governor Davis to interpose the sovereignty of the state to prevent integration. Board member Theodore Shepard, who proposed the resolution, saw it as the only way to keep the schools open on a segregated basis. After voting for the resolution, board member Matthew Sutherland, who persistently argued for realism, said that if interposition failed, the schools would either have to be integrated or closed. The board, he said, was at the end of its rope.

# CHAPTER III

## The Board Creates Community Support

At this low point, a new development changed the entire picture. Two days after the board's desperation became apparent, a group of people not previously identified with opposition to segregation formed the Committee for Public Education (CPE) and publicly said they wanted the schools kept open even if they were integrated. SOS had said the same thing, but now that CPE said it, the board could openly endorse token integration.* The effect of CPE's position was akin to that of an advance motorcycle escort that guarantees the safety of the marchers in a parade through hostile territory.

The difference between the memberships of the two organizations was critical. The chief difference was that there were no liberals in CPE, and that is what allowed the board to change its policy. Both SOS and CPE drew their membership from the upper-middle class, but the members of SOS favored integration and were relative newcomers to the South. CPE's members were, for the most part, native New Orleanians who had never favored integration. Interviews with CPE members revealed a vast gulf separating the two superficially similar groups. CPE members referred to SOS derisively as "a group of people who had no children in the public schools," the implication being that they had nothing to lose as a result of integration and had promoted it no matter how the children would suffer. By contrast, CPE was called a parents committee, a designation, one CPE member explained, that was made deliberately "to keep out the nonmoderates." One of CPE's founders, describing herself as a "segregationist but a law-abiding citizen first," said that, because of her known commitment to the public schools, she had been invited to the organizational meetings of SOS in the fall of 1959. She attended one meeting and was "shocked to find myself in such

* From this point on, all references to the board members, unless otherwise specified, will be to the four moderates.

company." (Nevertheless, the two organizations took identical stands.)

In terms of the kind of support the board needed, CPE's membership characteristics and public position fit so neatly that it is likely that the group was formed in response to requests either from the school board or from persons very close to the board members. The climate of opinion changed so much in precisely the way the board and Sam Rosenberg and Judge Wright wanted it to that one can surmise the efforts they took. After all, the people in CPE—not those in SOS—were friends and acquaintances of the board members, Sam Rosenberg, and Judge Wright. The Girls, the board members, the leaders in CPE, Sam Rosenberg, Judge Wright—these people were all well acquainted with one another and had been active in the school board elections.

Actually, these people were so intertwined and their actions so well concealed that it is difficult to say who did what. Who did what, fortunately, is not terribly important. What does matter is: The creation of CPE gave the board new options. Whatever the relation of the board to the creation of CPE, the board used CPE as any politician might use his constituency. In essence the board had begun to move back into politics.

During the tense months of May and June, two of the board members had been eager to resign and let someone else shoulder the city's burdens. The support of the politically respectable CPE gave the board a sense of legitimacy for the first time. This support not only kept the board members from resigning, but by the beginning of July, the board, which had been so desperate in the early part of June, had agreed to work to keep the schools open despite integration. This is the position the board had been struggling to arrive at throughout May and June. Until CPE's endorsement, it had never seemed possible of realization.

The very existence of CPE — a new institution — apparently emboldened some of the older institutions for, very shortly afterward, the Episcopal clergy of New Orleans, the clergy of the United Church of Christ, and all the pastors and elders from the Methodist churches in the area all came out for open schools.[24] The arrival of these new voices and others that followed in the summer broadened the constituency of the board members and stiffened their resolve to work for open schools, but the voices and the support they most needed in order to win over the community and prevent trouble—the support of the mayor and the elite—would be a long time in coming.

Throughout the summer of 1960, the federal courts and the State of Louisiana fought a running battle. In July, a state court enjoined the school board a second time from desegregating the schools.[25] The issuing of this injunction made it clear that the only way the school board could avoid conflict with both state and federal laws was to keep the schools closed.

On August 13, Mayor Morrison, under increasing pressure from his friends and supporters to do something to keep the schools open, finally uttered his first word on the subject, a request that Governor Davis disclose how he intended to keep the schools open and segregated. "The human and economic effects of closed public schools," Morrison warned, "could have a heavy impact on the community well-being."[26] A week later, Morrison said the city attorney had grave doubts about the Governor's ability to keep the schools open and segregated. Reminding Louisianans that the states' rights issue was settled in the Civil War, Morrison suggested that: "If we are going to lose the decision, inevitably, a small percentage of integration might be the answer in the situation instead of having lots of trouble and lots of mixing."[27] Then he lapsed back into silence.

Because of the additional powers given to the governor by the 1960 session of the legislature and because of the two state court decisions, the Negro plaintiffs in the *Bush* case went before the Federal District Court on August 16 to apply for a temporary injunction to restrain the governor, other state officers, and the school board from obeying the state court injunction and the statutes with respect to segregation in the public schools.

The next day, Governor Davis notified the city's Superintendent of Schools, James Redmond, that the Governor had superseded the school board and was now running the public schools of New Orleans. He ordered Redmond to open the schools on September 7 on a segregated basis.

### THE WILLIAMS SUIT

At this point, the efforts on behalf of the board moved into a new stage. The same day Governor Davis took over the New Orleans schools, August 17, a new suit was filed against him *(Williams v. Davis)* which gave a totally new aspect to the entire legal and political situation. This suit, filed by 30 *white* parents, was an application for a temporary injunction restraining the governor and other state officials from obeying the state court injunction and the state statutes with respect to segregation.* The stated fear of the white parents was that, though the Governor had specifically ordered Redmond to keep the

---

* Because the *Williams* and *Bush* suits sought essentially the same relief against the same parties, the court consolidated the cases. From that point on, the two were virtually synonymous, going up and down the ladder together from the District Court to the U.S. Supreme Court.

schools open, the Governor would use the authority vested in him by the various acts of the legislature to *close* the schools.

Though the legal questions in the *Williams* and *Bush* suits were similar, from a political point of view there was a world of difference between them. The filing of the *Williams* case marked the first public action taken by white parents in recognition of the danger to the schools posed by the state's activities. Once again, the CPE played a key role, instigating the suit, searching out white parents who would be willing to put their names to it, and finding an attorney to handle the case. After several attorneys refused, attorney Charles E. Richards agreed to handle the case. Many moderates were extremely fearful of harassment and even fearful for their lives; consequently, some of the most important activists in CPE did their work secretly.

During the interviews for this study, one such person expressed the belief, which he said was held by many in CPE, that the NAACP was deliberately "trying to lose the *Bush* case" so as to force the schools to close and thus "to dramatize the issue." Just three days prior to the filing of the *Williams* suit, a New York *Times* dispatch from New Orleans quoted unidentified "sources high in legal circles" who believed that the NAACP's pleadings did not "provide the court with an adequate basis for cutting through the barrier thrown up by state officials."[28] The white parents' suit evidently did provide such a basis. Thus the *Williams* suit was an attempt not only to prevent the governor and the legislature from closing the schools, but also to keep the Negro plaintiffs from losing the case (whether by design or otherwise) and forcing the schools to close.* In any event, the joining of the *Williams* and *Bush* cases in no way signified cooperation between the Negro and white plaintiffs—even though the two suits ostensibly sought the same relief. At no time did white moderates work with or for Negroes to desegregate the schools; the white efforts were strictly to keep the schools open.

The suit by the white parents was a vital move, for it added to the *Bush* case the interest of white parents in keeping the schools open *regardless of the outcome of the desegregation efforts.* Prior to the *Williams* suit, one was either pro-Negro and pro-integration or pro-white and pro-segregation. Now,

---

* Interviews with Negroes associated with the *Bush* case did not substantiate a "losing" strategy. Apparently, individual Negroes had commented that if the *Bush* case were lost, then the city would wake up and see how important the schools were, but I found no evidence that there ever was a strategy of losing the case. The CPE people also told the interviewer that this strategy was being used (possibly as a rationalization) by some of the economic leaders. "Let them [the legislature] close the schools," these businessmen are reported to have said to CPE people, "and let the citizens see how much harm would be done—then they will force the opening of the schools in quick order."

moderates could avoid this dilemma and opt for a third choice—keeping the schools open—which had the advantage of being a neutral principle between opposing factions. Thus, a move for "open schools," not a move to desegregate them, was the avenue upon which moderates finally entered the controversy. And this was the tack taken by the four members of the school board. The *Williams* suit was vital, not so much because it gave Judge Skelly Wright the grounds to strike down the state school-closing laws, but chiefly because it lent an aura of legitimacy to the board's now "moderate" position. The *Williams* suit was thus more of a political event than a legal matter.

The suit was so much the answer to the school board's prayers that again it seems likely that the *Williams* suit, which sought to enjoin the *school board* from obeying the state court injunctions, was in fact given behind-the-scenes encouragement and support by the four moderates on the board. (There is also some evidence—not substantiated—that Sam Rosenberg and even Judge Wright were instrumental in the preparation of the suit.) As with the formation of CPE, we see the board and its close allies creating options for itself—creating, in effect, a sub-elite that would endorse the board's position, and so making politics.

On August 27, the Federal District Court, awarding judgment for the Negro and white parents in both cases, (1) struck down as unconstitutional all of the acts of the legislature that would directly or indirectly require segregation of the races in the public schools, (2) nullified the seizure of the school board by the governor, and (3) ordered the board to get on with the desegregation of the schools.[29]

## THE BOARD MOVES

The formation of CPE, the suit by the white parents, and the unyielding position taken by the federal courts so greatly eased the course for the four members of the school board that they were now able to devote their energies to keeping the schools open. The four and the board's lawyer, Sam Rosenberg, met privately and set up a four-man Committee to Maintain Public Schools. This invention was a thinly disguised ruse to permit the board to hold meetings without having to have Emile Wagner present. At the first meeting, they decided to tell Judge Wright they were ready to comply. At a public board meeting the next morning Attorney Rault told the board there was nothing else they could do to fight the desegregation order. So, at a meeting prearranged by Rosenberg the four moderates met privately with Wright and told him they had made no plans to desegregate but were now ready to comply with his orders.

School was scheduled to open on September 7, little more than a week away, so the board asked the Judge to delay desegregation until November 14. The delay would give the board time to devise a desegregation plan, but they also sought it for two other reasons that were actually more important. First, a delay would mean that school would open on a segregated basis, and the difficulty of transferring would reduce the number of Negro pupils. The fewer the Negroes, the board members believed, the easier would be the transition. Second, with a delay, desegregation would not occur until after the November 8 election for a seat on the school board—the seat held by Matthew Sutherland, one of the moderates.

The idea for the delay, like the earlier idea to conduct the postcard poll of parents, was Lloyd Rittiner's. Despite the results of that poll and despite the still awesome silence of the community's leaders, Rittiner continued to believe that the majority of the city was in favor of law and order and the preservation of the public school system. Since Sutherland, who had come close to resigning a few months earlier, was now willing to run for reelection, the election would provide a good test of voter support for the stand taken by the moderates. Rittiner, with enough faith in the voters to be willing to run the risk of repudiation, wanted desegregation delayed until the moderate viewpoint of the city's voters could be shown.

Because the meeting with Judge Wright was so private that not even Emile Wagner knew it was taking place, the real reasons for the delay could be kept secret. On August 31, when the four members formally went before Judge Wright to request the delay, the only reason given was to allow the school staff time to prepare a desegregation plan. Judge Wright postponed the start of desegregation until November 14.[30] (Nineteen sixty was, of course, the year John Kennedy and Richard Nixon were campaigning for the presidency, and Judge Wright's delay was a great relief to both campaign staffs.) Attorney Rault resigned from his position with the school board, and Sam Rosenberg became once again the school board's sole attorney.

The board had made its decision—it would work for token integration. But now another decision had to be made—it had to come up with an integration plan. Like good politicians, the board members had found and utilized (and probably built up) support for their first decision. But in handling the second one, they seemed to forget what they had just learned. They acted as though their task had nothing to do with creating and selecting options and building public support—they acted, in other words, as if the decision had nothing to do with politics.

# CHAPTER IV

# School Integration — the "Scientific" Way

The public schools of New Orleans opened their doors on the usual segregated basis on September 7, 1960, leaving the board two months to prepare for the long-dreaded day. If the board's skill in building and utilizing community support for keeping the schools open suggested a certain recognition of the need for a constituency or a base of power, its actual integration plan cancelled any such suggestion. In drawing up a plan—which, in New Orleans' dual school system, meant selecting some Negro pupils to attend some white school or schools—the board absolutely refused to utilize the community support it now had. The idea of having or using a base of power was considered by the board members to be a dishonorable notion. Against the advice of friends, the board members steadfastly refused to consider such political considerations as: who would support what plan, where would support most likely arise, and where would the opposition be concentrated.

## SELECTING THE NEGRO PUPILS AND THE WHITE SCHOOLS: THE "MACHINE"

Trying to arrive at an "honorable," legally acceptable way of limiting the number of Negroes who would be entering the white schools, the board and the superintendent adopted, on September 26, a four-step administrative process for considering applications for permits to transfer. Forgetting or ignoring all political considerations, the board members wanted "objective," "scientific" decisions. Besides being nonpolitical and therefore "proper," objective decisions had the further merit of freeing the board members and the superintendent from personal responsibility for the decisions. Considering the enormous pressure on the four moderate members, their desire to put responsibility for the decisions as far away from themselves as possible is understandable. They had been receiving harassing, threatening phone calls at night, they were being referred to in the public press as the "four surrender members," old friends were shunning them, two members of the board were suffering severe financial losses to their businesses, and no one in a position of official responsibility in the community had risen as yet to support them.

A look at the administrative procedure devised by the board and the superintendent will indicate how carefully they tried to make the decisions objective. Applications from Negro parents were first considered by four assistant superintendents on the following basis: The information on the application had to be verified, the age of the child had to be checked, the consent of the parents had to be checked and the reasons given for the request examined, the nearness of the school to the child's home had to be considered, and also the availability of transportation.

Having passed this hurdle, the application for transfer was then subjected to consideration by psychologists, psychometrists, and the acting director of guidance and testing. This group of technicians—the board's scientists—examined the scholastic aptitude and the intelligence of the applicants. A crucial part of this step was the Metropolitan Readiness or Achievement Test, which had already been administered, as a matter of course, to all first grade pupils in the school system.

All the information thus compiled about each applicant was referred to a third screening group, this one composed of the assistant superintendent for instruction, the director of special services, the director of kindergarten-primary education, more psychologists, and what were called "visiting teachers." This group considered the effect of the new pupil upon the academic program, the suitability of the established curriculum for the particular pupil ("in terms of grouping within the class"), the adequacy of the pupil's academic preparation or readiness for admission to the school or to the curriculum, the psychological qualification of the pupil for the type of teaching and associations in the new school, the effect of his transfer upon the academic progress of the other students, the effect of his transfer upon "prevailing academic standards," the psychological effect upon the pupil, the home environment of the pupil, and the "maintenance or severance of social and psychological relationships with pupils and teachers."

Any applications still surviving were then considered by an administrative review team composed of the superintendent (for the first time in this process) the first assistant superintendent, the acting assistant superintendent for instruction, and the school system's medical director. This group was supposed to review all the information previously collected on each applicant and, in addition, to consider the choice and interests of the pupils, the possibility or threat of friction or disorder among pupils or others, and the possibility of breach of peace or ill will or economic retaliation within the community. Unfortunately, as will be seen shortly, the review team seems not to have considered the last two possibilities. It does seem to have followed faithfully the objective tests in the first three screenings, however.

As should be clear, the plan, which was taken from the Louisiana Pupil Placement Act, was designed to *exclude* Negroes. That any got by such a screening derives from the fact that the board *had* to find some, and it indicates there must have been some "cheating" on the system. The system or the plan, incidentally, was called by the board members the "machine," indicating the great extent to which they viewed the whole process as so scientific, objective, and mechanical that it was virtually computerized. Later, when they were criticized for their choices, the board members were to claim to the public and to the author of this study: "We didn't select the schools and the children; the machine did."*

As the final step in the selection process, the school board was to consider the findings of the administrative review team and then direct the superintendent to issue or not to issue a transfer for the pupil in question. However, the desire on the part of the board to avoid responsibility for the choices and to keep the choices "objective" was so intense that this last step was not followed. The four moderate board members urged Superintendent Redmond not to release the names of the Negro children even to themselves. In part, they were fearful of having the information released to Emile Wagner, who, they feared, might in turn release the names to elements in the community who might threaten or otherwise pressure the Negro families involved into backing out. (A fear, it developed, that was justified.) But the four moderates had been working covertly with Redmond anyway and could have easily obtained the information without letting Wagner see it. They simply did not want to know which Negro children and which schools had been chosen.

In the weeks after the plan was announced, a total of 137 Negroes applied for permits to transfer. While the school system was receiving these transfers, the board members were actively trying to enlist the public support of the community's elite. Help came from a well-known New Orleans attorney, who succeeded in getting five of the very top elites to meet with school board

---

* A claim that is not strictly true since the board *instructed* the "machine" to find no more than ten Negro pupils.

president Rittiner at the end of September. Because the men refused to be seen with Rittiner in public, it was a secret meeting. Rittiner argued, as many others had previously, that any chaos or disorder would be harmful to the city, and he called on these social and business leaders to take a public stand in support of the board's efforts to achieve a peaceful token desegregation. These leaders tried to bargain with Rittiner, offering their assistance to protect the city from trouble only if the board would separate the first grades by sex and keep the toilets in the schools segregated by race. Rittiner saw nothing wrong with separating the first graders by sex—all the New Orleans schools had at one time been so divided—but he rejected the condition regarding the toilets. Aside from the probability that it would be rejected by Judge Wright, the very idea of such a condition being imposed by these particular men seemed to him simply ridiculous. The meeting ended without any promises of support from the businessmen. On October 10, in an apparent attempt to make integration more palatable to these men, the board resolved to keep all integrated classes separated by sex.

On the same date, the board made a fatal decision: That all accepted applicants for transfer to white schools must have test scores equal to or above the median *for the school to which they were applying.* Since this rule was crucial in deciding not only which Negro children but more importantly which white schools would be integrated, it is important to understand how it was administered. It had been a long-standing practice in the New Orleans public schools to give to all children, white and Negro, the Metropolitan Readiness or Achievement Tests during their first week in first grade. The class median was based on the scores from each school's first grade for the previous five years. In 1960, the usual testing policy was followed during the first week of school in September. The Negro pupils who had applied for transfers were assigned to take additional tests, which were administered by psychologists who reported also on the behavior and dress of the children and their parents.

The choice of the white schools was to be determined by finding a school whose first grade median was *low enough* to admit the Negro pupils. Some people (both inside and outside the school system) urged Redmond and the board, as a *first* step, to select schools where the white parents and children would accept the Negroes and *then* to find Negro pupils who could fit in. But Redmond and the board would have none of such, in their opinion, subjective criteria. The board members insisted, and still did four years later in 1964, that the best educational experience for the Negro children could be achieved in a classroom where they would not feel inferior (a position which reflects the board's belief that the Negroes were really not ready for integration). The practical result of the board's policy—and its refusal to entertain any "subjective" considerations—was that it chose to desegregate the schools that gave every appearance of being the worst possible ones.

In the first place, only two schools were chosen, which meant that it was easy for the segregationists to concentrate their fire. Secondly, both schools—William Frantz and McDonogh No. 19—were in the same neighborhood, making it even easier for the segregationists. In addition, the neighborhood was generally poor, with a concentration of white working class families and lower class families in housing projects, the group most likely to be hostile to Negro advances.

But these schools were poor choices for political reasons as well, for they are both in the most neglected section of the city, the ninth ward. The ninth ward has always been the last to get street lights, the last to get paved streets, and the last to receive the myriad other city services that other sections are able to obtain more easily—and now it was the first to be integrated! Politically, socially, and economically, New Orleans has long been dominated by the Anglo-Americans, who live uptown—i.e., "above" (west of) Canal Street—and the Creole French, who live in the French Quarter. In the nineteenth century, the area "below" (east of) the French Quarter was the immigrant truck-gardening section of the city, composed of Germans, Italians, and non-Creole French.[31] Though many of these people have achieved middle class status, their section is still politically weak. This is the section where the ninth ward is. To the residents of the ninth ward, the decision to desegregate two of their schools, and none in any other part of town, seemed motivated by pure malice, and even the moderates in the ward were furious.

It is only necessary to add that the ninth ward of Orleans Parish is the next-door neighbor to St. Bernard Parish, which is led by archsegregationist Leander Perez, and that one of the two schools, McDonogh 19, is itself only a few blocks away from St. Bernard Parish. It was easy for Perez to hire pickets to disturb the two schools and to make the schools in his parish the haven for whites boycotting the two integregated schools in New Orleans.

Had the board been willing to make a "political" choice of schools rather than a "scientific" choice, much of the difficulty could have been avoided. Board members told the interviewer this analysis was merely hindsight. But they were urged *at the time* to choose schools where Negro children would be likely to be accepted by the whites. Most significantly the PTAs of at least two schools actually petitioned the school board in October requesting that Negro children be sent to their schools. The two schools, Wilson and Lusher, are in middle and upper class neighborhoods near Tulane University.

This gesture by the PTAs was not an invitation to have Negro children transported across the city to a nice white neighborhood to attend school and then back again to their own neighborhood. New Orleans has had residentially integrated neighborhoods for three hundred years. Negroes have lived even in the most expensive neighborhoods. One of the most militant Negro leaders of New Orleans lives between two ardent white segregationists.[32] Only since World War II has there been tight residential segregation, and this has occurred only in the new residential subdivisions. The middle and upper class whites who requested the school board to send Negro children to their schools were speaking of the Negro children who were living near them and attending all-Negro schools just a few blocks away from the all-white schools. In fact, Negro children were living right across the street from one of the two white schools whose PTA had requested Negro students.

A final point in this connection is worth noting. The president of SOS said in 1961 that the open schools campaign had made little progress in the neighborhood of Frantz and McDonogh 19 "because we found few civic groups through which to work."[33] In the neighborhood of the Wilson and Lusher schools, however, there were many civic groups which were already on record as supporting open schools; in fact, this was the home of the chief support the school board had received for keeping the schools open. Had these been the schools to be integrated, trouble may still have arisen but at least the school board was on notice that there were white parents there who were willing to accept the children.

Considering the board members' own long run objectives, then, they could not have made worse choices. It is easy for us to say now that with any political sense they should have realized they were courting disaster. Yet we must try to understand that the circumstances in New Orleans had destroyed the confidence of the four men. It was difficult for them to trust their own judgment or their own senses. Their friends would not even talk to them in public. Because it was "objective" and "scientific," the "machine" gave them confidence, and they truly believed they were making the right decision. And we must remember that they did not feel they were choosing the schools; as they saw it, their sole decision was to let the "machine" choose the schools. Furthermore, their actions were fully supported by the reform ideology. To the board members, it seemed that they were doing nothing more than deciding a question "on its merits," i.e., without political considerations, and that is what they were recruited and elected to do. In developing its plan, the board was truly "out of politics."

## THE CONTINUING CAMPAIGN FOR COMMUNITY SUPPORT

While the school board and the staff were still developing their screening procedure, and well before any announcement had been made about which schools were to be integrated, the open schools campaign focused on the reelection of Matthew Sutherland to the school board. The election was set for November 8, the same day as the Kennedy-Nixon presidential election. The Independent Women's Organization (IWO), an important element in the Girls, publicly came out for open schools on August 3 and joined forces with the women of the Committee for Public Education (CPE) in asking the elite and Morrison to support Sutherland.

Having largely held themselves aloof from the reform movement and from the city's politics, the elite were not easily moved by these appeals. But Morrison was more vulnerable because, as a member since 1936 of the good government movement in New Orleans and as the city's reform mayor since 1946, he had enjoyed the close friendship and vigorous support of many of the people who were now beseeching him to support the open schools movement. Still, he would not move. Some of his closest friends and admirers are still bitter today over his rejection of their appeals. He refused to endorse Judge Wright's desegregation order, and he refused to endorse the board's decision to comply with it. His few statements about the schools were weak and equivocal. Behind the scenes, he did make one attempt to swing the elite out into support of open schools, but when they rebuffed him—some refused even to discuss the subject with him, others were more polite—Morrison reportedly turned to two confidants and said, "Well, if those s.o.b.'s aren't going to do anything, I'll be damned if I'm going to stick my neck out!"

But the issue could not be ignored. The emphasis on open schools rather than integration permitted "respectable" elements of the community to take a public stand in support of the board for the first time. In June, it was CPE; during July and August, various Protestant clergy, a few union locals, IWO, and the Junior Chamber of Commerce. It must be emphasized that no white group made an effort in 1960 to win popular acceptance of Judge Wright's orders. Even those who spoke for keeping the schools open (except for SOS) stressed that they were *for* segregation. And the school board itself did not switch from resistance to compliance until the issue changed from integrating the schools to keeping them open. The moderates were so forceful in framing the issue in this way that by October the segregationists were put on the defensive and compelled to say that what they wanted was to keep the schools segregated *and open*. And near the end of October the elite made their first tentative behind-the-scene steps toward support of peaceful desegregation.

During the month of October, reports were circulating that Governor Davis was going to call a special session to try to halt school desegregation in New Orleans. The five businessmen who had met with Rittiner in September (and who then were not willing to commit themselves publicly to the board's support) journeyed twice to Baton Rouge to urge Davis not to interfere. They feared state interference would stir up trouble in New Orleans. Since the elite were not ready to endorse peaceful desegregation, the meetings with Davis were kept from the public. These men had been important Davis supporters in the 1960 election, and Davis was aware of their economic power. They left his office under the impression that he had promised not to call a special session, but they (and others) later told the interviewer that Davis never gives a direct answer to a question. The school board members knew of the effort made by these men and were suitably grateful, but the board needed *public* support from them.

On October 27, the school board announced that it had granted transfer permits to five Negro pupils, all girls. Their names were not revealed; nor were the white schools identified. When Governor Davis saw that the school board was really going to comply with the desegregation orders, he sprang into action, and, on October 28, called the legislature into the first of several special sessions, to begin on November 4. To prevent New Orleans legislators from preparing a defense, Davis maintained strict secrecy as to the contents of the bills he would submit. Rumors quickly swept the city that the Governor was going to "interpose" the legislature between the federal government and the school board. The legislature, so this rumor went, would block integration, or remove the school board, or close down the schools. This latest threat to the schools, combined with Davis's rejection of the plea by the business leaders, finally served to bring some of the elites out into the open.

On November 1, in a front page editorial, the New Orleans *Times-Picayune* endorsed the candidacy of Matthew Sutherland.

> Mr. Sutherland, in our opinion, has proved himself an ardent opponent of forced integration. He has backed every effort by the school board to have set aside court orders to end segregation. Nevertheless, opposition to Mr. Sutherland seems to be based on the school board's adoption of the state's placement law which was designed to meet the emergency that now exists. As far as we can see the board had no option. After losing some 35 appeals to the courts of one kind or another, the federal court order had to be recognized. The board wanted, of course, to keep the schools open and segregated. It has had to accept limited segregation [sic] under the pupil placement plan. It has no authority to close the schools

if it wanted to. The Legislature and the Governor can close the schools (if the closing is applied to the whole state). But none of Mr. Sutherland's opponents . . . has a definite plan to keep them open and fully segregated.

Sutherland's principal opponent, John Singreen, was endorsed and supported by the White Citizens' Council. His stand indicates how the framing of the issue in terms of closing the schools or keeping them open had put the die-hards on the defensive. In answer to the editorial, Singreen wrote:

> The sole issue is, are the voters willing to accept integration now, or are they going to fight now for their rights. The four surrender members of the school board have already approved integration . . . and it will be a reality on November 14 unless each parent, each voter . . . make up their [sic] minds to fight for their constitutional rights . . . .
>
> Governor Jimmie Davis was elected by the people of Louisiana to keep the schools open and segregated. The people should trust the governor and the schools will remain open and segregated, and our own. . . .[34]

Emile Wagner endorsed Singreen and, referring to the postcard poll of parents, declared that Sutherland had violated that "mandate" of the people.*

The two other candidates for Sutherland's seat on the school board were Caryl Vesy, who labeled Sutherland a defeatist for believing (according to Vesy) that the only choice was between compliance or a total loss of the school system, and Mrs. Marie McCoy, who thought there should be a mother on the board and declared that if the people wanted the schools closed, she would close them.

The stand of the four moderates on the board was well expressed by Sutherland. He reiterated his advocacy of segregation, but said, "We must face the issues as they are, not as we would have them to be. The question is, do we want public education or do we want economic chaos?"[35] Seeing no other way to keep the schools open, he would comply with the federal court orders, "but I would favor anything the Legislature can do to keep the schools open and segregated."[36] The last plank in this platform was a reliance on the Pupil Placement Act as an effective way of limiting and controlling integration. After fighting off forced integration for eight years, the four segrega-

---

* A few days later, Wagner, running as an unpledged elector in the presidential election, called for the defeat of both Nixon and Kennedy as a way of stopping integration. Integration, he said, would be a disaster because tests had shown "40% of Negro students verged on moronic and ranged on down to imbecilic." *Times-Picayune,* November 8, 1960, sec. 3, p. 18.

tionists on the school board were now reluctantly going to admit a few Negro children, but only to keep the schools from being closed and only under conditions which would limit and control the number of Negroes. They nonetheless hoped the legislature would come up with a way of keeping the schools open and segregated. In short, their position was a tightrope act, treading the only politically safe passage to desegregation in the emotional climate of New Orleans and Louisiana.

On November 4, the first day of Governor Davis's special session, a committe of 100 important business and professional men, headed by an executive committee of 18 of the city's most influential citizens—the elite, at last—publicly endorsed Matt Sutherland. The endorsement, "for the future of our children and for the continued growth of New Orleans as a major industrial center in the South," made no mention of the fatal issue except for an indirect reference to the closing of the schools: "Our struggle with the Soviet Union . . . makes it imperative that the education of our children not be stopped or interrupted. . . ."[37] The day before the election, this committee ran a three-quarter page ad in the *Times-Picayune* listing 98 names and signed, "Business and Professional Men's Committee for Sutherland." (See Appendix III.) Though the only message on the page was, "We believe that we and our children will all have a better future if Matt Sutherland is elected to the School Board," the "best people" in the city were now at least advocating Sutherland's election *and* contributing money to his campaign.

### THE SPECIAL SESSION

On the same day, everyone finally learned the details of Davis's legislative package. As soon as the bills were distributed to the legislators, the House, according to plan, voted to suspend the rules and, without discussion, immediately sent the bills to the administration-controlled judiciary committee. Only one representative from New Orleans, Maurice Landrieu, objected on the floor to the suspension of the rules, and he was voted down, 93 to 1. Another New Orleans representative, Salvador Anzelmo, described the administration "steamroller": "Twenty-nine bills were dumped on my desk, and within 15 minutes referred to a committee, without us having any opportunity to read or digest those bills."[38] Anzelmo said many members of the House objected to the procedure but dared not speak up for fear of being branded integrationists. The New Orleans delegation decided, in typical New Orleans fashion, not to work as a unit, but to let each man work on his own. This is how Landrieu was left to make a one-man stand against the suspension of the rules. Throughout the session, Landrieu, with occasional help from some of the others, notably Anzelmo and Senators Robert Ainsworth and Adrian DuPlantier, risked his political career to fight these bills. (Yet even Landrieu felt compelled to assert his attachment to segregation and to claim that he "wouldn't know a Communist if I saw one." "But," he said, "I tell you here and now if I had to choose between accepting five Negro children, or closing the entire public school system, I will stand for the open schools.")[39] The steamroller was so effective that within five days all 29 bills had been passed by both houses and signed into law by Governor Davis.

Davis's entire package depended upon Bill Number Two, which purported to interpose the sovereignty of the state between the federal government and the school board. The rest of the package was an arsenal of additional devices to prevent integration. (See Appendix II.) The federal court which reviewed these Acts at the end of the month succinctly summarized their function in this fashion:

> In order to forestall any effective integration order for this school year, present enrollment on a segregated basis is "frozen" and transfers are forbidden (Act 26); but, for the future, any school under an order to desegregate is immediately closed (Act 22), whereupon the local school board ceases to exist (Act 21); to carry out these directives . . . the state police are given additional powers and placed under the orders of the Legislature (Act 16), and if demonstrators are needed, they may now be recruited among the students who are no longer compelled to go to school (Act 27); to assure that an integrated school does close, the new legislation provides that if it continues to operate it shall enjoy no accreditation (Act 20), teachers shall lose their certificates (Act 23), and the students themselves shall receive no promotion or graduation credits (Act 24). . . .[40]

But if the interposition bill could not stand up in the courts, then the whole structure would collapse.

The school board members—helplessly bounced around by these events like a rubber ball—pledged their full cooperation if the governor succeeded. "The only thing I am against," Rittiner said, "is the closing of schools. As an elected official I feel it is my duty to provide public education, if possible on a segregated basis but, if not, on an integrated basis."[41] Emile Wagner, on the other hand, professed confidence that passage of the bills would keep the schools open and segregated, and he taunted his four colleagues, "It is to be regretted that the school board did not have more confidence in the governor. If it had it would not have walked hat in hand to a federal court and capitulated so that now it is bound by its word to the court to integrate."[42]

Since the Davis legislation chiefly affected New Orleans, a new issue arose— "home rule." Desegregation, politically speaking, was a one-sided issue: Everyone was against it. The second issue, keeping the schools open, brought out many who had been silent before. Even Davis's men were forced to argue that they were for keeping the schools open. But the attack on New Orleans' "home rule" brought out the resistance of legislators and others who had been silent on both previous issues. Not even the issue of keeping the schools open had drawn Mayor Morrison into the fray. Morrison's co-floor leaders in the House opposed very few of the 17 bills (out of the 29) directly affecting the New Orleans school system. In the New Orleans House delegation, only Landrieu voted against all 17 of them. Of the other members of the delegation, Anzelmo voted against 16 bills, George Tessier 13, Peter Murtes 11, and Kenneth Barranger 7. Morrison's two floor leaders, Edward LeBreton and Joseph Casey, voted against only three and one respectively. Four of the city's House delegation voted against only two of the bills. Nine of the city's delegation supported all of the bills.[43]

However, when the legislature wanted to have an eight-man committee take over the New Orleans schools, LeBreton one of Morrison's men, introduced an amendment to have the committee be composed entirely of New Orleans legislators. "We've come a long way," said LeBreton, "toward getting our school board out of politics. I'm against only one thing—your taking our school board away from us."[44] LeBreton was put on the legislative committee, but his amendment was defeated, and this is the issue that finally stirred Mayor Morrison. On November 8, he told the press:

> I have been shocked to learn that the House . . . rejected a proposed amendment by Orleans legislators seeking local control of its own affairs. . . . It is just as wrong for Mr. Garrett [upstate Claiborne Parish] to try to run our Orleans school affairs as it is wrong for the U.S. Supreme Court to dictate to the people of Louisiana. . . .
>
> It looks like home rule is taking another licking.[45]

It was stimulating in New Orleans to learn that Morrison could be shocked by what was going on in Baton Rouge, but his shock was misplaced and came too late to have any effect on the outcome of the proceedings. He had made only two tepid remarks—on August 13 and 21—expressing his concern for keeping the schools open, but, as the performances of his floor leaders reveal, he did nothing to stop the legislation which would close the schools in his city.[46] Furthermore, Morrison waited until after all the school-closing bills had been passed before speaking up. He was not trying to prevent a legislative committee from taking over the schools; he merely wanted the committee to be composed of New Orleans legislators. The integrity of the school board was not even considered.

In sheer voting strength, a united New Orleans delegation could easily have been outvoted, but one wonders whether Governor Davis would have even attempted to go so far had official New Orleans presented a solid front of opposition. It is one thing to knock over a few representatives obviously acting on their own, but to go against the united opposition of the mayor of the state's largest city, his political organization, and all his state legislators might have required a greater amount of force than Davis would have wanted to expend on a single issue. Such an encounter, even were he to win, might have cost him more than the issue was worth to him. The second special legislative session that Davis was to call provided a good illustration of the power New Orleans could exert. A bill clearly aimed at Morrison would have made mayors and police chiefs subject to removal from office if they assisted in the execution of federal court orders, e.g., by protecting children to and from desegregated schools. In the judiciary committee, Davis had sufficient numbers to report any bill favorably, but this bill was attacked by mobilized New Orleans forces and was quashed in the committee.

## THE COMMUNITY CHOOSES

On election day—ironically, the same day the Louisiana Senate passed the bills—the New Orleans voters rejected the die-hard position and elected the moderate Matt Sutherland by a wide margin.

1960 SCHOOL BOARD ELECTION, ORLEANS PARISH[a]

| Candidate | Vote | Percentage of Vote |
|-----------|------|--------------------|
| Sutherland | 55,493 | 55.6 |
| Singreen | 31,367 | 31.4 |
| Mrs. McCoy | 10,145 ⎫ | |
| Vesy | 2,831 ⎭ | 13.0 |

* Official figures from Secretary of State for the State of Louisiana.

On that day, also, the *Times-Picayune* finally abandoned its neutral stand.[47]

We conclude that closing of the public schools would be worse than the damage to the schools which we believe will be an inevitable result of forced integration.[48]

It was not much of an endorsement, but the paper did at least have the courage to make its statement before the election results were known.

Sutherland's victory meant that the community was ready to accept token integration. From that moment, the school board members dropped their passive role as victims of circumstances beyond their control and became actors bent on achieving peaceful desegregation.

The outcome of the presidential race also brought significant changes in New Orleans. It brought in the federal government. Heretofore, the federal government's involvement was limited to steps taken by the courts. Political observers in Washington understood that United States Attorney General William Rogers had been eager to enter the *Bush* case but had been held back by President Eisenhower. Republican strategists feared that Nixon would lose the state if New Orleans became "another Little Rock."* But Nixon lost the state despite the President's caution.[49] As President, Kennedy was to be much more active than Eisenhower in Southern desegregation, but the changes did not have to await Kennedy's inauguration. Just two days after the election, the United States District Attorney in New Orleans (a Southern Republican who is said to have hated the local Democrats more than he hated integration) went before Judge Wright and obtained orders restraining all Louisiana sheriffs, police chiefs, and mayors from interfering with federal court officers in the discharge of their duties attendant to school desegregation.**

* In this instance, "another Little Rock" refers not to violence and closed schools, but to federal activism. Eisenhower had sent troops to Little Rock in 1957.

** "To this moment," writes J. W. Peltason in a chapter on New Orleans in *Fifty-Eight Lonely Men* (N. Y.: Harcourt, Brace & World, 1961), "the Department of Justice had refrained from actively entering the case." This is an accurate observation, but, strangely, only seven pages earlier, Peltason had written, "From the very outset of the New Orleans crisis, President Eisenhower's Attorney General Rogers had been an active participant." That sentence appears in a paragraph whose footnotes refer to November 13, hardly the very outset of the crisis. Whatever the cause of Peltason's confusion on this point, his entire chapter is loaded with errors which flow from two misconceptions of the New Orleans situation. His first misconception is his belief that the issue was primarily a legal problem; the second is his belief that the school crisis did not begin until mid-November 1960. With this picture in mind, Peltason concludes: That the New Orleans school board "was not alone . . . Mayor deLesseps S. Morrison and the responsible citizenry backed the board . . ."; that "moderates . . . controlled New Orleans" and had the support of the Roman Catholic Church. Peltason

In electing Sutherland, the community had made a choice, but time was running out. On the morning of the 10th of November, four members of the legislature's eight-man committee (provided for by the Davis legislation) to run the New Orleans schools arrived at the New Orleans board of education building accompanied by three armed state police and stripped the school board of its authority. The chairman of the committee, Risley Triche, announced that he knew of no transfer of students that had been approved.

A few hours later, CPE's attorney, Charles E. Richards, appeared in Judge Wright's court at the request of the white parents in the *Williams* case asking for an order restraining the legislative committee from forcing the schools to close. Judge Wright set November 18 for a hearing on the constitutionality of the statutes passed in the special session and issued orders temporarily forbidding implementation of these statutes.

At 6 P.M., Sam Rosenberg told the board members they were back in control of New Orleans' public schools. With this assurance, the board formally authorized the transfer of the five Negro girls into two allwhite schools.

That night Governor Davis called his second special session. On Saturday, the 12th, State Education Superintendent Shelby Jackson declared a state holiday for the 14th, but on Sunday morning (the 13th) Judge Wright issued restraining orders against the holiday.

On Sunday, November 13, the legislature, in a session beamed across the state on TV, fired Redmond and Rosenberg for refusing to identify the Negro girls and, instead of the special committee, placed the entire legislature in charge of the New Orleans schools. No judge had ever enjoined an entire legislature, but that evening, Judge Wright, who had been watching the session on TV, signed preliminary restraining orders against Governor Davis and *all* members of the legislature.

Even more significant than this shattering of legal precedent is the fact that these restraining orders were requested by the Orleans Parish school board. The four men who, in June, had asked the Governor to interpose state sovereignty to prevent integration, were now sufficiently strengthened by community support to request federal assistance in preventing state interference with desegregation.

---

can sum up the situation with these words: "New Orleans was not to be another Little Rock with a lonely judge, a few Negro school children, and an embattled school board forced to face angry segregationists without civic support or federal assistance." As evidence of the civic support that sustained the board, he cites a newspaper ad which appeared on December 14, 1960, and a testimonial dinner which was not held until January 30, 1961.

But the board's integration plan was so bad that the gains so laboriously achieved by the formation of CPE, the filing of the *Williams* case, and by Sutherland's decisive victory were all but thrown away. Support had been created uptown, and the schools were being integrated downtown, where integration was hated and feared. With chaos in the offing, the board had turned to a "computer." And when the computer came up with a politically disastrous answer, the board simply ignored the political considerations. Though the board members and other moderates were still campaigning for public support from the mayor and the elite, at mid-November the only thing that could have prevented chaos would have been a change in the board's integration plan. No change was made, and the militant segregationists took command of the situation. The board had been kept out of politics; the price for this triumph of reform principles was to be a breakdown of social control in the city.

# CHAPTER V

## Mardi Gras

On November 14, 1960, four frightened Negro girls (the fifth had withdrawn her application), three at McDonogh 19 and one at Frantz, became the first of their race in the Deep South since the end of Reconstruction to attend classes with whites below the college level. Until the Negro children actually arrived at school that morning, the board's plan had been a closely guarded secret, and the people of New Orleans did not know which schools were being desegregated. The discovery that both schools were in the ninth ward set off immediate reverberations.

As soon as word spread that morning, many parents of the white pupils came to take their children home. By the end of the week, every white child was withdrawn from McDonogh 19, and every white child except two were withdrawn from Frantz. The two exceptions were the daughters of Mr. and Mrs. James Gabrielle and Reverend Lloyd Foreman. Except for one brief period in January 1961, no white pupil returned to McDonogh 19 during that school year. The father of the children who temporarily broke the boycott at McDonogh 19 was fired by Walgreen's and had to leave town when no one else would hire him. At Frantz, because of the courage of the Gabrielles and Reverend Foreman, a few more parents brought their children back, and the boycott at that school was never total.

On Tuesday the 15th, the day after school opened, roving packs of truant teenagers tried to break into the two desegregated schools, but were turned back by police. Eleven boys were arrested, but all were released without prosecution. During the day, Governor Davis called on the people of New Orleans to "restrain their emotions and above all things keep a cool head."[50] That night, Willie Rainach, Leander Perez, and other segregationist leaders spoke to a mass rally of 5,000 at the municipal auditorium. Rainach called for a "scorched earth" policy.

Bring the courts to their knees . . . Let's empty the classrooms where they are integrated. A day lost can be made up; a week, a year lost is not fatal. . . . But once bloods are mixed, that is forever fatal.[51]

Perez, the poet laureate of the racists, called for demonstrations against the NAACP, the Communists, the "Zionist Jews," Judge Wright, and "the real culprit, malefactor and double-crosser—the weasel, snake-head mayor of yours." Perez concluded:

Don't wait for your daughter to be raped by these Congolese. Don't wait until the burr-heads are forced into your schools. Do something about it now.[52]

The next day, a mob variously estimated at between 1,000 and 3,000 swept through the New Orleans civic center and into City Hall and then marched on the federal courts and the board of education. As the mob steamed down Carondelet Street toward the board of education, one member of the board and some members of the staff watched in terror from the roof of the building. Police turned the mob away from the board of education building with fire hoses, but it continued to roam through the business district throwing bottles and stones at Negroes in buses and cars.

After the street demonstrations, Mayor Morrison appealed on television for an end to violence. His talk stressed the damage that could be done to the "image" of New Orleans "as a thriving center of commerce and industry" if the "ugly irresponsible incidents such as took place today" continued. At the same time, he maintained his dissociation from the school board and Judge Wright. "I should like to repeat," he said, "that the New Orleans police department has not and is not enforcing the federal court order relative to school integration."[53] He and the police, he explained, were only trying to maintain law and order. Morrison's close friends and associates in the good government movement—including Skelly Wright—were aghast at his failure in this address to call for obedience to the law of the land and support of the moderate school board. That evening, after Morrison's talk, Negro teenagers went out on the streets seeking revenge for the stonings. One Negro boy was knifed, two white men were shot by a Negro, another white man was shot by a roving band of Negroes, and many other whites were beaten by gangs of Negroes. That night, police made 250 arrests, mainly of Negroes.

The next day, the Mayor called an urgent closed-door meeting of leading citizens to discuss the crisis. One hundred and sixty business and professional leaders attended the meeting and issued a statement calling on citizens to do their part to preserve peace and order. The statement, signed by most of the very top elite, commended the mayor, the police, and the city council for preserving law and order, but made no mention of the school board.* Two days earlier, the Young Men's Business Club had also spoken out against the demonstrations, but it, too, failed to support the school board, expressly tabling a resolution to do so.[54]

Some people (including Superintendent Redmond on November 16) have praised the Mayor and his police superintendent for their "coolness" and their ability to prevent the spreading of the riots. But what permitted the violence to get started in the first place? The point is that the white violence in New Orleans had the tacit approval and support of the community. Neither the mayor nor the elite, in their calls for peace, had called for support of the school board or of the law of the land. Further, though Morrison said the segregationists had the right to demonstrate so long as they did not disturb the peace, the police permitted whites to make the most flagrant disturbances of the peace. Demonstrators physically and verbally abused the Negro and white children attending the two desegregated schools, yet the police did not stop this abuse. When the police turned back the mob at the board of education building, a woman grabbed Police Chief Giarrusso and pleaded, "Chief, help us, not the United States Government." Giarrusso replied, "We'll help you if you do it in an orderly manner, but we are not going to let you take over the city."[55]

Governor Davis, of course, had set the tone for defiance of the law—which thereby encouraged the rowdiness and abusiveness—and Morrison and the elite of New Orleans had passed up every opportunity to create a countervailing tone of respect for law and order. Little wonder, then, that the general appeals for peace by Morrison and Davis were ignored.

At McDonogh 19 and especially at Frantz a huge crowd gathered every morning to taunt, shove, heckle, threaten, spit at and upon, the Negro girls and the few white children who dared go to school in violation of the boycott. This crowd consisted mainly of women, wives of working class and unemployed whites in the ninth ward and neighboring St. Bernard Parish. (One physical indication of the ninth ward problem was the sign carried by one demonstrator, "If you are poor, mix; if you are rich, forget about it; some law!")

On the 29th of November, the "coolness" of the police permitted a mob of 400 to follow Mrs. Gabrielle and her daughter all the way home from

---

* Since the unruly demonstrations by whites were continuing, this praise of the city officials made no sense—except that the praise came the day after the police moved swiftly to stop *Negro* outbursts.

school and swarm over them, shouting obscenities. Threats poured into the family, windows in the house were smashed, and Mr. Gabrielle, who worked for the city as a meter reader, was frequently told by his sadistic supervisor that his wife had been shot. Gabrielle finally quit his job, and, when he was unable to get another one, the family moved out of the city in mid-December. Mrs. Gabrielle had lived in New Orleans for 35 years. The Gabrielles, it should be noted, were neither liberals nor intellectuals (nor Jews nor Communists); they were "unexceptional" people doing what they thought to be a perfectly ordinary act—sending their child to school. That their ordinary act can be called courageous—that this act made them very exceptional—is a measure of how the world had been turned upside down in New Orleans.

That the Mayor and the police simply *would not* protect the Gabrielles utterly depressed and frightened decent New Orleanians. It meant that men and women were free to act out their revengeful fantasies right in the streets. With madness in the streets, the people whose support of open schools had been so carefully elicited were frightened back indoors.

## MADNESS IN THE LEGISLATURE

On the 14th of November, the legislature, having learned that the school board had requested court orders to restrain the governor and the legislature, accused the board of complicity with the federal court and the NAACP and angrily removed from office the four "traitorous" members of the school board. By the time school opened the next day, however, Judge Wright had issued further orders putting the school board back in business.

The legislature's second special session began on the 15th of November with both houses commending the "brave fight" of the parents who removed their children from the desegregated schools. In addition, the legislature (1) declared illegal all acts of the "now defunct New Orleans School Board" and warned all banks and businesses not to do business with or honor checks of nor make loans to the "old" school board; (2) directed that the funds of the Orleans school board be transferred to the legislature; and (3) provided for a system of education expense grants for children attending nonprofit, nonsectarian, nonpublic schools. It also fired Redmond and Rosenberg again for not disclosing the names of the Negro girls and the white schools they would attend.

This was an angry session. Every legislator who dared even to question these bills was charged with "treason." These tactics even forced Representative Landrieu to return to the calendar a modest resolution calling on state officials to use their influence to prevent violence and urging parents to express their indignation peacefully.

The attack on the funds of the schools was by far the most menacing step taken by the legislature. In the previous school year (1959–60), the state had provided almost sixteen million dollars of the school board's 28.7 million dollars, 55.6 per cent of the total revenue.[56] Of the remainder, 42.5 per cent came from local property taxes levied by the school board. (The school board receives no funds from the city except for a trivial part of the sum paid by the New Orleans Housing Authority to the city in lieu of taxes.) Though it would appear that the legislature could thus hold up "only" 55 per cent of the school board's revenues, the legislature could in fact hold up much more than that, for the school board does not have the power to collect the taxes it has levied. These taxes are collected once each spring by the city. Consequently, the board is forced each year to borrow money from banks to pay the operating costs of the school year, and these loans cannot be entered into by the board without state approval. For the coming school year, the board would have to negotiate loans totaling $12,746,000, but the immediately pressing need was a loan of $2,100,000 to meet the November 23 payroll. Unsurprisingly, the state Bond and Tax Board refused to authorize the school board's request for this loan. One bank, the Whitney National, which continued to cash the school board's checks, was removed as fiscal agent for the state.[57]

The financial pinch was so bad and the first week of desegregation had been so disturbing that on Friday, November 18, the harassed school board asked the federal court for a further delay of desegregation until the state and federal governments settled the issue of sovereignty. This was the school board's 39th appeal of federal court orders.[58] Sam Rosenberg told the judges:

> From a practical point of view, the board is reaching a point that regardless of the orders of this court, we soon will be unable to operate. We are running out of money and the banks won't give us any. And rightfully so, probably—they don't know who's running the schools.[59]

The same day, the white parents in the *Williams* case asked the court for an injunction against further interference by the state. The court took both requests under advisement.

On November 22, Superintendent Redmond announced that the school system could not meet its teacher payroll since its application for a loan had been turned down by the state. The next day, the legislature authorized pay for all Orleans Parish school employees except for the administrative staff and the teachers at the two desegregated schools. The teachers at Frantz and McDonogh 19 were not paid until after Christmas.

In October, the board had had to reject a $10 million bond sale because the rates of the low bidder were the highest the board had ever received. A spokesman for the low bidder warned the board the desegregation crisis might force the rates even higher. As a result of the unusually high rate, the board rejected all bids and announced that its building program, already one year behind schedule, would have to be set back another year.[60]

Sniping at the board from all angles, the state got an injunction on November 14 from the state court in New Orleans restraining the board, Redmond, and Rosenberg from interfering with "the Legislature's schools" in Orleans Parish. But Rosenberg was able to invoke a federal law to transfer this case to the federal court, where Judge Wright promptly nullified the state court decision.

On November 30, the federal court in New Orleans announced its decision on all the matters that had come before it during the month. The court struck down the Interposition Act as an illegal defiance of constitutional authority. The sole purpose of the legislative package, the court held, was to defeat the constitutional right of Negro children to attend desegregated schools. Therefore, the whole package was unconstitutional.[61] Once again, the court enjoined over seven hundred state and city officials from interfering with what the federal court called "the school board's proposal" to admit Negroes to previously allwhite schools. In addition, the court turned down the school board's request to delay the desegregation. On December 12, the United States Supreme Court, holding that the legal issues involved in the case were "not matters of doubt," upheld the District Court's decision.[62] The November 30th decision of the District Court, though by no means the last decision in the case, was nevertheless the climax to the legal battle.

The battle between the federal courts and the state of Louisiana was now utterly predictable. In all, Davis called five special sessions extending all the way to February 26, 1961, but at each succeeding session fewer and fewer meaningful acts were passed. The oratory in these sessions grew more heated, and the denunciations of Judge Wright, the Supreme Court, the federal government, the school board, and all the real and imagined enemies of segregation and white supremacy grew more vehement, but the legislators knew, after November 30, 1960, that every act they passed to interfere with school desegregation would be struck down by the federal courts. In all the federal court decisions in the eight year history of the case, there was never so much as a single dissenting opinion. Eventually, even the legislature revolted against Davis when he proposed, on December 17, a one-cent sales tax increase to finance the start of a grant-in-aid private school program.[63]

### ENFORCING THE BOYCOTT: THE BATTLE OF THE STREETS

Perhaps *because* legislative interposition had failed, the street disturbances in New Orleans grew more intense after November 30. The real battle was now being fought in the streets, and the battle was focused on perfecting the white boycott. The abuse of the mob against the parents and children continued. The Louisiana Advisory Committee's report to the United States Commission on Civil Rights describes the situation:

> During the last days of November, Reverend Lloyd Foreman and Mrs. James Gabrielle, who had continued to take their children to the Frantz school, were subjected to abuse and physical violence by the mob in front of the school. This, coupled with the fact that several parents in the Frantz school area had appealed to S.O.S. for help in returning their children to school, led to the organization of a volunteer "carlift," run by parents from the uptown section of New Orleans, which transported the children to school in relative safety. The "carlift" began on December 1.[64]

Given some sense of safety by the carlift, a number of parents began sending their children back to Frantz. On December 6, a total of 23 white children attended Frantz, but the number was never again to climb that high.

> The car carrying Yolanda Gabrielle was stoned and manhandled by the mob. Later in the week, it was pursued for two miles by a truck which had tried to ram it. Until Wednesday, December 7, the drivers and the women who escorted the children into the school were subject to the vilest sort of shouted abuse from the daily-assembled crowds. On December 7, the police guarding the school pushed the crowd behind barricades a full block away from the school. The crowd then dispersed to roam the streets of the Florida Housing Project, where many of the children live.[65]

A new wave of threats, stonings, and other harassments quickly reduced the number of white students to eight. On December 8, the White Citizens' Council distributed a list of all the volunteer drivers, describing their cars and showing their telephone numbers. This stopped the carlift. Two parents, Marion McKinley and Marvin Chandler, withdrew their children after threats on the lives of themselves and their families and warnings that they would lose their jobs. The McKinleys, with two children at Frantz, reported that their windows were broken nine separate times.[66] Another parent,

Everett Poling, removed his child after his tires were slashed and his family was threatened.[67]

> Parents were subjected to an organized telephone campaign of threats and abuse. Their houses and other properties were stoned, as was one of the mothers of a child at Frantz. The jobs of the fathers were threatened; four of them lost their jobs. . . . The volunteer drivers were threatened with death, arson, disfigurement . . . With the exception of a couple of juveniles alleged to have stoned [the mother of a white child] no one connected with the demonstrations was arrested, nor was the mob in front of the school dispersed or told to move on.[68]

Starting with December 9, the federal marshals began transporting the white children who wanted to attend Frantz. But by this time the parents were too frightened; the number of whites attending Frantz was kept at ten or fewer for the remainder of the school year. Emile Wagner sued Superintendent Redmond to obtain the names of all the pupils enrolled at Frantz. (This suit was filed November 25, and on December 7 the state court ordered Redmond to give Wagner the names. But Redmond did not release the names until February 1961, when the Louisiana Court of Appeals affirmed the decision of the lower court.[69]) No one was under any doubt as to why Wagner wanted the names.

With the transfer of the battle from the legislature and the courts to the streets, the New Orleans crisis now became an international spectacle, with a huge press and TV corps covering the street battle. For millions of Americans, the ugly scenes from New Orleans were digested along with dinner during the Huntley-Brinkley newscast every evening. Many national journals and papers carried a running box-score on the number of whites attending Frantz.

One of the sharpest observations of this scene came not from a journalist sent to cover the story, but from John Steinbeck, who happened to be traveling through the South in late 1960. Dressed in an old jacket and a British navy cap so no one would think he was a reporter, he joined the crowd in front of the Frantz school one morning.

> The crowd was waiting for the white man who dared to bring his white child to school. And here he came along the guarded walk . . . leading his frightened child by the hand. . . . A shrill, grating voice rang out. The crowd broke into howls and roars. . . .
> No newspaper had printed the words these women shouted. It was indicated that they were indelicate, some even said obscene. On television the sound track was made to blur or had crowd noises cut in to cover. But now I heard the words, bestial and filthy and

degenerate. In a long and unprotected life I have seen and heard the vomitings of demoniac humans before. Why then did these screams fill me with a shocked and sickening sorrow?

The words written down are dirty, carefully and selectedly filthy. But there was something far worse here than dirt, a kind of frightening witches' Sabbath. Here was no spontaneous cry of anger, of insane rage. Perhaps that is what made me sick. . . . Here was no principle good or bad. . . .

The crowd behind the barrier roared and cheered and pounded one another with joy. . . .[70]

Steinbeck found it hard to believe he was in New Orleans.

Where were the others—the ones who would be proud they were of a species with the [father who braved the crowd]. . . . Perhaps they felt as helpless as I did, but they left New Orleans misrepresented to the world. The crowd, no doubt, rushed home to see themselves on television, and what they saw went out all over the world, unchallenged by the other things I know are there.[71]

Where were the others? Why were the mayor and the elite willing to let the city be misrepresented?

Morrison steadfastly denied any responsibility. In November, he blamed the trouble on "outside agitators" such as Rainach and Perez.* In December, Morrison found a new scapegoat—the outside press. Since the demonstrators were obviously enjoying their press clippings and their performances on television, Morrison claimed that the crowd was merely performing for the press. On December 4, he asked for a three day press moratorium on the school protests. This request, he said, "comes from the heart of a public official who has spent most of his life trying to build the economy and the good name of New Orleans." He explained that the "impression" of turmoil *created* by the press coverage was bad for New Orleans business, "and it is a damage that we are suffering *completely without fault on our part*."[72] (Emphasis added.) When the reporters refused to stay away, he asked them to form a small pool to cover the story. The reporters agreed to form a pool if he would reduce the number of demonstrators proportionately, but Morrison refused.

---

* During the schools' annual week-long Thanksgiving vacation (November 21 through 25), Perez threw open the public schools of St. Bernard Parish to New Orleans' boycotting pupils. Since St. Bernard was so close, the parents found it easy to accept Perez's offer. The legislature later reimbursed St. Bernard Parish for the expense of educating the pupils it took in. In January, Redmond estimated that of the 1,019 pupils who had enrolled at McDonogh 19 and Frantz, 601 were in St. Bernard schools, 132 were in various other public and private schools, and apparently 286 children were receiving no formal education whatever. *Southern School News*, February 1961, p. 6.

The question of whether the reporters were the cause or the effect of the trouble stirred our New Orleans respondents as did few other questions. The elite vehemently denounced *Time,* Huntley and Brinkley, and the outside press in general, and, four years later, were irritated when the interviewer used the word "crisis." The elite and some moderates told the interviewer they saw *Time's* newsmen and television cameramen rehearsing the crowd on how and when to yell. An article in *The Nation* the following year agreed with Morrison and cited the New Orleans coverage as one of many examples where newsmen, by their presence, make the news.[73] Daniel Boorstin went even further and called the New Orleans disturbances a "pseudo-event" created by the press.[74] But this argument is based on the mistaken assumption that, if there had been no newspaper and television coverage, the die-hard segregationists would have been perfectly content to stay at home and permit the schools to be integrated.

To the people who had to endure the jeers, the stonings, and the loss of jobs, there was more than what Morrison called an "impression" of turmoil in New Orleans. The broken windows in the houses of the people who dared send their children to school attested to something much more real than Morrison and the elite were willing to admit existed. The windows were not broken in front of the television cameras; the men were not fired from their jobs in front of reporters; the threatening phone calls were not made in front of photographers; Emile Wagner did not sue for the children's names and addresses as a publicity stunt. All of these moves had only one objective—to enforce the boycott. The only "show" part was the cheering section at the school, but even this was bestial enough to scare most parents and children away.

Robert Coles, a psychiatrist and writer, observed the crowd each morning and also had many visits with one of the Negro children and one of the white women who shouted epithets and threats at the children. What Coles learned from this Negro girl and the white woman substantiates the view of this discussion that the events were real and not created by the press. The screams and threats heard were *not* broadcast on television or written in the newspapers. " 'You little nigger, we'll get you and kill you,' was a commonplace," says Coles. But one concrete threat terribly frightened the child. "Spoken in a high-pitched but determined voice, its words were always the same: 'We're going to poison you until you choke to death.' " This little girl developed a strong fear of many kinds of food. Coles's description of the white woman who shouted this particular threat further dispels the notion that the crowd at the school was there just to see themselves on TV. The woman, according to Coles, was weary, very sad, very frightened, and poor. Her education stopped at eighth grade, she had more children than she could cope with, and she had a wayward husband who drank heavily. She felt that her life was cheated and impoverished. And she very much feared and hated Negroes. When the school was integrated, she felt that Negroes would dispossess her children. Clearly, no one needed to coach this woman on when or how to shout at the Negro children.

But she did need an opportunity to behave as she had at the school. This opportunity was not given to her by the press but by the city officials and community leaders who permitted the existence and behavior of the mob. Coles could find no special reason in this woman's personality or her history for her having joined a mob and behaving as she did while in it. Her hatred for Negroes seemed to Coles to be "conventional . . . , not unlike those [sic] of other people who never have joined mobs. She was undoubtedly influenced by the attitude of her city, its hesitant police and politicians; that is, by the fact that there was a mob, that one *was* allowed to form and daily continue its actions." Seeing this woman some time later, Coles noticed that her children were now in the desegregated school. She still hated Negroes, but, "deprived of the outlet of the mob, she goes on, strained . . . but law-abiding."[75]

By dissociating himself from the school board and those who were trying to help the children get to school, Mayor Morrison led the city's malcontents to believe they could act without restraint. Morrison's excuse for not stopping the mob was: "My job is to maintain law and order . . . not to run the schools."[76] Incredibly, he said this at a time when a breakdown in law and order was keeping children from attending the public schools of his city. Morrison's callous approach to the issue is illustrated by his behavior with regard to the Mardi Gras a few months later. Every year the first important Mardi Gras event is the "landing" and parade of the Zulus, a group of Negroes who wear blackface, hand out coconuts, wear grass skirts, and, in general, dress and act like savage buffoons. The integration controversy had aroused New Orleans' Negroes and led to the city's first Negro sit-ins at Canal Street lunch counters. Many Negro leaders felt that Negro participation in the Mardi Gras, and especially in the Zulu parade, would be demeaning at such a time. Their efforts to prevent the Zulu parade were described in a *New Yorker* article.[77] Under pressure, the Zulus reluctantly voted to cancel the parade. Morrison was alarmed. Word of the Zulu cancellation would add fuel to rumors that the Mardi Gras would not be held and would give the "impression" of racial strife in the city. The Zulus explained to Morrison that they were eager to have the parade but were fearful of hostile acts by resentful

Negroes and segregationist whites. Morrison and the police chief guaranteed the Zulus they would be fully protected along the parade route—and indeed they were. A huge contingent of zigzagging motorcycle police kept the Zulus completely isolated from the audience that lined the route. A friend of Morrison's told me that Morrison not only confirmed the story but thought it was a great joke on those who had criticized his failure to protect the Negro and white children at the integrated school.

The behavior of members of the White Citizens' Council is crude and predictable and therefore, in a sense, easily dismissed. But in New Orleans, as Morrison's cynical humor attests, the behavior of the Citizens' Council was of a piece with the behavior of the whole community. Indeed, the behavior of the elite and of Morrison and of some of the friends of the board members—since much was expected of them—was worse than the behavior of the Citizens' Council. When a city is so permeated by fear that decent men cannot talk with their friends on the street, when businessmen are too frightened to speak for moderation, then the social fabric of a city is all but destroyed.

### AN END TO MADNESS

Morrison's refusal to protect and fight for the few individuals who were trying to preserve the good name of the city (and the elite's refusal to insist that he do this) cut deeply into the city's ability to promote itself as a progressive, indeed, a liveable city.

The day after Morrison described himself as "a public official who has spent most of his life trying to build the economy and the good name of New Orleans,"[78] a page one story in the New York *Times,* under the byline of Claude Sitton, was headlined, "New Orleans Rift Takes Trade Toll."[79] This toll, Sitton reported, was apparent in Morrison's public utterances and in the private remarks of business and civic leaders. Business leaders declined to speak for the record (in good New Orleans fashion), but they privately estimated hotel and restaurant trade to be about 20 per cent off the customary rate. Hotel cancellations nationally were averaging 10 to 12 per cent, but in New Orleans the figure was higher than 25. An earlier story by Sitton on November 28 had noted sharp declines in department store sales as well as in the tourist-dependent restaurants, night clubs, and taxis. One New Orleans executive told Sitton, "Canal Street merchants told me that their business for November—as of November 25—was the worst in memory, even including the depression."[80] (Canal Street is the city's central shopping section.) The same executive reported to Sitton that one major department store's sales dropped 35 per cent and the sales of another more than 40 per cent. Sitton learned that business leaders were greatly disturbed but "reluctant to make any public attempt to resolve the problem apparently out of fear that this might bring economic sanctions from the Citizens' Councils . . ."[81] The *Times-Picayune* did not report these developments, and a New Orleans reporter told me that New Orleans newspapermen became avid readers of out-of-town papers to follow these economic developments.

Around this time, the American Veterans Committee in New York suggested that tourists avoid the Mardi Gras while the turmoil in New Orleans streets continued. The *Times-Picayune* angrily answered in an editorial.

> Admittedly, New Orleans is caught in racial tensions. That, however, is a situation not of our own making. It was thrust upon us illegally and incited callously by extraneous forces that care not a whit what harm is done the city. . . .
>
> The city has conducted itself commendably during these trying times and has preserved its dignity. . . .[82]

The wording is almost identical to Morrison's disavowal of responsibility, and, also like Morrison's remarks, the editorial reveals a belated concern for the city's reputation.

But the businessmen could not remain silent forever. On December 14, the same day on which the *Times-Picayune* printed its editorial on the Mardi Gras, 105 business and professional men of New Orleans ran a three-quarter page ad in the newspaper appealing for an end to threats and street demonstrations and for support of the school board. (See Appendix IV.) This was the closest the board had come to receiving support from the elite, and the ad contained the name of a man who was generally believed to be the pinnacle of the social and business life of the city. However, he was the only member of what can be considered the top elite to sign the ad. The ad was distributed throughout the nation in an effort to counteract the bad publicity which had curtailed business in New Orleans.

Unfortunately, the ad came much too late. The businessmen could have said the same things *prior* to the crisis. Instead, they waited until an economic slump hit the city and law and order had broken down. An article in the New York *Times* Magazine in November 1960 quoted an unnamed Southerner as saying:

> Several months ago a business leader from Little Rock came to New Orleans to talk with some of the merchants and industrialists about the potential for damage to business that lay in this school situation. Many of the businessmen wouldn't even discuss the

subject with him and the rest were very cool to the case he was trying to make for preparation to avert crisis.[83]

By December 14, obviously, some of them had learned for themselves, and the ad, though lacking the signatures of most of the top elite, signalled at least the beginning of the end of the elite's passivity. Their long silence, however, had made their task of bringing peace to the city doubly difficult. Still the ad was the beginning of the end of fear in New Orleans.

To counteract the bad publicity caused by the street disturbances and to put an end to rumors that the Mardi Gras would not be held, Morrison (ever quick to defend his city) announced on December 15 that the Mardi Gras, scheduled for February 14, was definitely on and would be the biggest ever. Morrison also wrote to all major cities that there was no friction in New Orleans and urged people to come to the Mardi Gras.

Meanwhile, the school board's problems mounted. On December 22, the day before payday, the legislature had adjourned without releasing funds for the salaries of 4,000 teachers and other employees of the Orleans school system. Some of the funds were released in January, but again not for Redmond or Rosenberg or the teachers at the two integrated schools. Federal court orders directed at various banks released some money. (Despite the earlier court orders, the banks had refused to honor pay checks written on the school board's deposits.)

With the state Loan Board still refusing to sanction loans in anticipation of local taxes, Mayor Morrison, finally deciding to help save the schools, appealed in January to property owners to pay their taxes in advance. Leading businesses, including the city's public utility and the newspapers, responded and paid in advance, one more sign that the business leaders were no longer content to sit and watch the school system flounder. The taxes paid in advance helped pay school personnel who had not been paid for two months. (Nevertheless, the financial condition of the school system was still weak when the 1961–1962 school year began. The state board was still refusing to authorize bank loans.)

In January, the school board was attacked by yet another source. The Louisiana School Boards Association, of which Matthew Sutherland was the president, had voted in December to support the governor and the legislature in the school crisis. In January, two days before Sutherland's term as president of the association was to expire, he and the three other moderates on the Orleans school board were ousted by the association by a vote of 210 to 9. The legislature promptly passed a resolution thanking the association.

All along, the board members and the superintendent believed that all their difficulties could be handled if the mayor and the leading businessmen would only support the board's efforts. Throughout the troubled months, the women in CPE, IWO, and the League of Women Voters had worked unceasingly to involve the elite. It was the women who had obtained the signatures for the ad endorsing Sutherland and the December 14 ad. And on January 30, 1961, the efforts of the women culminated in a huge testimonial dinner at the Roosevelt Hotel for the four board members and the superintendent.

To understand the significance of this public dinner, one must recall that during the height of the crisis, the board members were not only reviled by their opponents, but, in many cases, shunned by their friends. One board member said that old friends would pass him in church and furtively whisper to him, with their eyes averted, that he was doing a good job. He told these friends the best thing they could do for him would be to speak to him openly on the street, but this they refused to do. Such was the venomous atmosphere in the city. Another school board member told the interviewer two leading businessmen had phoned him during the height of the crisis and said they would like to meet him at a restaurant in the French Quarter to discuss ways of helping the board. He was overjoyed and replied that if he could just be seen having lunch with them that would be the biggest help they could give. But they would have lunch with him only in private. At lunch, they offered to try to get the banks and the legislature to release the money needed for teacher's salaries, and they made a genuine effort to do so even though they failed. But the school board member was correct; what he needed most from them was a public affirmation of support. Only with that could the board begin to solve its problems. Behind-the-scenes talks were of no avail; the problems could not be solved until the governor, the legislature, and the people of New Orleans knew that the civic elite of the city was standing firmly and openly behind the school board.

On January 30, however, 1,650 citizens came to the dinner to pay tribute to the board members for the sacrifices they had made to preserve public education in New Orleans. One of the organizers of the meeting made a short address in which he said a recent New York *Times* editorial had asked, "Where are the Southern moderates?" This gathering, said the speaker, is our answer. "We are here at the Roosevelt Hotel." When the main speaker, Harry Kelleher, a prominent attorney who is one of the top elite, was introduced, the master of ceremonies said: "If the face of the mob on Carondelet Street is our worst face, our speaker tonight represents our best face—the aspect with which we would like to face the nation and world at this time."[84] The things Kelleher said were incontestable, but for a school board member to hear someone like Harry Kelleher say them in public was to awake from a nightmare. "[We] are confronted now," said Kelleher, "with the question of whether we believe our public school system is worth preserving. . . . We must consider whether we believe in due process of law . . . , and second, whether we believe in public education. This country and the South cannot afford to go backward." Citing the "gallant" fight the board put up to resist desegregation, Kelleher said the four men "have stood steadfast and discharged their full duty to us and to the children of this community. It behooves all of us to support these four honorable men. . . . We owe them our everlasting gratitude."[85]

It is evident from Kelleher's words that the financial crisis was not the only reason so many business and professional leaders had come to this testimonial dinner. Their failure to aid the board members for so long had cost them something of their humanity. The testimonial dinner was a great act of social reconciliation; at long last, the community was having dinner in public with the board members. In the brief speech of thanks delivered by board member Riecke, one can feel the euphoria coming off of the board members.

> We believe . . . very strongly that the people of New Orleans elected us to the school board not only to administer business affairs of the school system but to improve and perpetuate public education in the city of New Orleans. . . .
> We are going to do exactly that, come hell or high water. . . .
> With the help of the taxpayer, and with the help of good citizens like you who are supporting us, we cannot fail.[86]

The January testimonial had finally provided the needed public display of confidence and support. From that point on, though the boycott was still effective, though the school system's finances took another year to straighten out, the school board and the superintendent knew that their problems, serious as they were, were manageable. It was no longer a sign of communistic leanings if you talked to a school board member on the street. At last, the school board's efforts had legitimacy. Events of the remainder of the school year and of the following year proved the school leaders were justified in their confidence. Though the patient was still ill, the fever was broken. The crisis was over.

# Part Two

## CHAPTER VI

## School Integration — The Political Way*

### NEW ORLEANS ABANDONS SCIENCE

In the midst of the city's crisis—on November 3, 1960—one member of the city council embarrassed his fellow councilmen by introducing a resolution asking the legislature not to close the New Orleans schools. Legally, the city council was not involved, and most of the councilmen wanted to stay out of the controversy. But since it was just a resolution in favor of keeping schools open, it was embarrassing to argue against it. Pinney and Friedman called this session a "fist-pounding debate," giving the impression that the council was angry at the legislature, but the fist-pounding was directed at the "trouble maker" who introduced the resolution. Finally, the seven-man council passed it, 4 to 2, the seventh man having ducked out of the room while the others were not looking. Later, one of the council called the man who ducked out "the smallest man" on the council.

He was also the council's president—Victor H. Schiro, Jr. Two days after ducking out of the politically embarrassing council session, Schiro chaired a meeting he had called of local businessmen and city and state officials to discuss the loss of industry from the New Orleans area. Schiro was able to get some of the top business leaders to this meeting, and he told them they would have to act or "wake up some day and find that New Orleans is no longer a place that attracts industry, but just a nice place to spend a weekend."[87] Schiro reminded them that it had been almost three years since a major industry had moved to New Orleans, and he urged them to act to improve the business climate of the city.

* The historical material in this chapter is based almost exclusively on newspaper and magazine accounts.

In July 1961, when Morrison resigned as mayor to become the United States Ambassador to the Organization of American States, the city council appointed Victor Schiro to succeed him. Schiro does not have the reform "mentality," he is not interested in reform, and he is precisely the kind of politician the reformers despise. Many deride him as "just a party back." Yet this man is the one who led the city to its successful desegregation of the schools in 1961. This is no paradox, no reversal of form. Because he was a politician rather than a reformer, he provided what Morrison and the reformers could not—a political government for New Orleans. Yet so closely do reformers adhere to their reform ideology rather than to policy, that in 1962, after Schiro had achieved what the reformers had been trying to do—the peaceful desegregation of the schools—they ran a candidate against him in the race for mayor.

Schiro followed the modern politician's dictum that good government is good politics. He was determined that if the city had to desegregate, it would be done in a manner that would avoid another economic setback and would bring praise to his administration. In August, Schiro told the public: "I am putting all on notice that law and order will be maintained at any cost."[88]

Schiro, of course, was not acting alone. His strong statements appeared simultaneously with a series of moves and statements by the city's business and professional leaders. On August 22, the Chamber of Commerce, which had been notably silent in 1960, stated:

> Business climate greatly affects the economic development of our area, and when it is unfavorable, it retards our development through loss of industry, trade and employment. New Orleans . . . has been subjected to adverse publicity . . . regarding incidents that involve friction between the races.

The Chamber statement went on to ask

> the assistance and support of all citizens in the maintenance of law and order and in the avoidance of all situations and incidents that could be magnified and publicized in a manner that would create an unfavorable image of our city. . . .[89]

On August 31, 315 civic and business leaders ran a full-page advertisement in the *Times-Picayune* that, for the first time in the city, called for peaceful desegregation of the schools. (See Appendix V.) The ad carried three times the number of signatures that had appeared on the December 1960 ad and contained nine of the top ten elites.* This ad went much further than had

* See p. 80 for a description of the method by which the elites were identified.

any of the 1960 statements by the civic elite. The opening sentence said that "public education . . . must be preserved; . . . and the dignity of our city upheld. . . ." The text of the ad said what had never before been said by any New Orleans leader—that the city of New Orleans should be free to operate in compliance with the orders of the federal court. "Preservation of law and order in Louisiana," the statement continued, "requires compliance with the final decisions of the United States Supreme Court; any other course would result in chaos." (See Appendix VI for a comparison of the December 1960 and August 1961 ads.)

In addition to these public statements, there were private assurances to the school board of the support of some of the top civic leaders. It is highly probable that such support meant that the elite had some voice in the school board's decisions. When asked for their support the previous year, the elite had set preconditions. Since the choice of schools in 1960 was the fatal error, one can surmise that it was in the choice of schools that the elite made its suggestions or conditions for support in 1961.

At any rate, in September 1961 the school board, with the mayor and other community leaders behind it, behaved quite differently. Although the board still used the Pupil Placement Act and still put the Negro applicants (only 66 this time) through the same rigorous screening, the results of the process were different from what they had been the previous year. This time, the *board* selected the neighborhoods and the schools to be desegregated and did not leave these important decisions up to the "machine." Thus did the board move towards making decisions on the basis of political considerations such as which neighborhoods would most likely support or at least tolerate desegregation.

Since few Negroes applied to the schools in the "good neighborhoods," the board "lowered" its standards and made the test the median level for the school system at large.* The result was that the board was able to select four additional schools to receive Negroes, and two of these schools were in areas of higher-income whites. These two schools, Wilson and Lusher, were the ones whose PTAs had requested Negro pupils in 1960.

There was no need to worry about the outside press in 1961 because there was no need for a large contingent of the press to come to the city. Schiro instructed the police not to allow any crowds to form around the schools, and

---

* The board members called this a "lowering" of standards, but in effect it represented a raising of expectations. That is, the board set the original standard in part because it believed Negroes could not perform well in a "good" school. The new standard assumed that Negroes could respond to a "good" school.

Police Chief Giarrusso took the assignment as a professional challenge. He proudly stated he would need no help from other law enforcement agencies. "We have an obligation to ourselves," he said, ". . . to prove that we are capable of handling our own affairs. . . ."[90] Giarrusso is the same police chief who, in 1960, allowed the mobs to surround and harass the pupils at the Frantz school. Apparently, he was responding to different commands from the new mayor.

The school board met with Giarrusso and Mayor Schiro, and afterwards all three gave public assurances of the safety of all children attending school. In all of these actions, one can see the public participation by Mayor Schiro backed by the business leaders of the city. Schiro was performing for a national audience, trying to restore the dignity of his city so that once more it could attract industry.

Desegregation in September of 1961 went smoothly and peacefully. Police set up 60-men teams at each of the six schools and barricaded an area extending one block in each direction from the schools. At the end of the first day, Mayor Schiro told the city:

> I am most grateful to the people of New Orleans for the manner
> in which they accepted this mandate of our federal government
> and courts.[91]

His wording, in the sharpest possible contrast to Morrison's public statements in 1960, makes it clear that in the second year, peaceful desegregation was the legitimate position.

When the civic leaders were asked in 1964 and 1965 about their silence in 1960, they consistently replied that there had been no crisis. All the city had, they said, was a handful of paid demonstrators getting their names in the papers and their faces on television. The whole thing, they insisted, was distorted and exaggerated by the press in order to sell more papers and magazines. That the elite knew the situation had been considerably more serious than that is revealed in their behavior in preparing the city for the second year of desegregation. Their complete change in 1961 is a corroboration of the judgment that they should have spoken up in 1960.

Still, the major difference between what happened in 1960 and what happened in 1961 was the establishment of a political government by Victor Schiro. In 1960, the city's mayor had been silent, maintaining that "running the schools" was none of his business. By implication, that meant that what happened to the schools was not the *city's* business. In 1961, the new mayor made peaceful school integration the city's concern. This was most likely the crucial determinant for peace in 1961, for other important steps followed from this change, including the school board's employment of political criteria for the selection of the Negro pupils and the white schools to be integrated. But not only the means were changed; the goals themselves were different. In 1960, the board's goal had been the avoidance of personal responsibility for the selection of the pupils and the schools, a goal that dictated the reliance on scientific, technical criteria for selection. In 1961, its goal became nothing less than the successful and peaceful desegregation of some of the city's white schools. This was a political goal, i.e., one that sought a change in the public policy, one that could be achieved only by careful attention to considerations of constituencies and bases of power and persuasion of the public. The very absence of a *city* policy on school desegregation in 1960 had compelled the board to avoid personal responsibility for decisions. By contrast, when the mayor in 1961 set the political goal of achieving peaceful desegregation and publicly called for support of the board and compliance with the federal law, the board had no need to be timid. It could boldly choose the schools on the frankly political basis of which ones could be successfully desegregated.

## ATLANTA

As is generally known, Atlanta successfully desegregated some of its schools in 1961 without any racial strife. Atlanta's success is a confirmation of the judgment that New Orleans' success in 1961 derived from the reestablishment of a political government in the city. Atlanta's mayor, school board, school superintendent, and police department worked hard for two and a half years to mobilize the community. Following this political leadership, numerous individuals and groups representing a "moderate" position on integration spoke up frequently, publicly, and early on the need to achieve peaceful desegregation.

Atlanta's success was not inevitable. For many reasons, observers of the South in the 1940s and 1950s would have been justified in predicting that New Orleans would have handled the problem successfully and Atlanta unsuccessfully. New Orleans, as we have seen, was considered the chink in the wall of the South's resistance to change. New Orleans was Catholic, tolerant, cultured, and residentially integrated. Atlanta was a "Jim Crow" city. Furthermore, the obstacles to the peaceful handling of racial issues were as great in Atlanta as they were in New Orleans, and in some cases, the obstacles were greater in Atlanta. Both cities were at the mercy of the governor and the legislature, but New Orleans was at least fairly represented in the state legislature. Atlanta, on the other hand, was a victim of Georgia's notoriously discriminatory county unit system. With approximately 14 per cent of the state's population, Fulton County (Atlanta) had less than 2 per cent of the representatives in the legislature. And unlike Louisiana where, because of the stable bifactionalism, race was ordinarily not a factor in election campaigns, Georgia had long been the scene of race politics, with men consistently elected on a platform of keeping the Negro in his place. Louisiana's Longs were popular with the Negroes; Georgia's Talmadges were race-baiters.

In addition, Atlanta, like New Orleans, had received a large influx of rural people more in sympathy with racist rural legislators than with the racial progressives and moderates from the city. This influx had almost caused the defeat of Atlanta's moderate Mayor William Hartsfield in 1957. He was re-elected by only 3,000 votes, winning largely on the returns from the Negro wards.

In both cities, it should be added, the Catholic hierarchy disappointed moderates by desegregating the parochial schools *after* the public school system had paved the way.

As in New Orleans, the Atlanta school system held a relatively low place on the scale of the community's priorities. In 1961, a bond issue to finance many projects, including expansion of the school system, was defeated. To get it passed on a second try, the mayor appointed a committee dominated by business influentials to pare down the program and establish quotas for the projects included in the bond drive. Though the schools were in a severe financial condition, this committee cut the heart out of the proposed school program, and this time the bond issue passed.

In the 1958 race for the Georgia governorship, Ernest Vandiver's opponents charged that he was soft on segregation because he had permitted Negroes and whites to be served barbecue in the same line at a political rally. To exonerate himself, Vandiver made extravagant promises to preserve segregation. His principal campaign theme was that not one Negro child would attend school with whites while he held office. He promised that state troopers and guards would be used to keep the schools segregated. When he was inaugurated in January 1959, he was ready with bills to create a state-supported private segregated school system.

Largely because of the rural legislators and Vandiver, who was considered much more adamantly opposed to school integration than Louisiana's Davis or even Faubus or Governor Almond of Virginia, Atlanta was generally believed to be a potentially worse situation than Little Rock or New Orleans. Georgia's General Assembly had passed a series of laws which would shut down the entire Atlanta public school system if any school in Atlanta was desegrated. The laws would not only cut off state funds, but also prohibit the county and the city from raising taxes for the support of any school in the district. Publisher Ralph McGill wrote: "There does not seem much hope of avoiding closing the public schools."[92]

The Atlanta desegregation case was filed in the federal court in January 1958, and in June 1959 Judge Frank A. Hooper ordered the Atlanta school board to present a desegregation plan by December.

Here, the similarity between the two cities ends. Unlike New Orleans' mayor, Atlanta's Mayor Hartsfield gave his city real political leadership. In 1957, he had told a group of white civic leaders that, "If Atlanta loses control of peaceful relationships, we are gone. It is of special importance to downtown businessmen. . . ."[93] It is not necessarily true that peaceful race relations are of special importance to downtown businessmen; we must remember that Mayor Hartsfield was speaking to them and may simply have been trying to alert them to their interest in the matter. But what was indubitably of special importance to *everyone* in Atlanta was that their mayor had taken a forceful public stand on the issue. In November 1958, when an Atlanta attorney proposed selling the city's schools to private parties to prevent desegregation, Hartsfield immediately and publicly condemned this proposal. He termed the closing of the public schools unthinkable and argued publicly that a single day's shutdown would do irreparable damage to Atlanta. He demanded that Atlantans be given a chance to vote on whether they wanted to keep their public schools open even though desegregated. Hartsfield's political leadership made all the difference between New Orleans and Atlanta. In striking contrast to New Orleans, where everyone had remained silent with the mayor, the early commitment and strong public stand of Atlanta's mayor encouraged others to speak up and made support for the open schools position respectable in Atlanta. Very shortly after Hartsfield's statement, manifestos in support of the mayor came from 311 ministers and rabbis, 419 doctors, two-thirds of the faculty at Emory University, and Parent-Teachers Associations from all over the city. In New Orleans, the mayor was waiting for the rest of the community to make the issue safe for him; in Atlanta, the community spoke up after the *mayor* had made integration, if not a safe position, at least a respectable one.

Significantly, the public concern in Atlanta for keeping the schools open arose *before* there was a final federal court decision in Atlanta's desegregation case. By contrast, public leaders in New Orleans were still debating whether to come out' publicly for keeping the schools open seven months *after* the school board had been given a desegregation plan by the federal court. In November 1958, the possible loss of the schools was already the leading news story in Atlanta. The leaders of New Orleans ignored and evaded the issue until it burst upon them in the form of street riots.

Early in 1959, a group of Atlanta housewives organized and called themselves Help Our Public Education (HOPE). They raised funds for the open schools campaign, but their principal contribution was in keeping the subject out in the open. Like SOS in New Orleans, HOPE took no stand on integration and confined its efforts to keeping the schools open. But unlike SOS, HOPE was able to raise the subject and get an audience because its efforts had already been legitimized by the city's political leaders. HOPE even organized throughout the state. The obscene telephone calls that HOPE's members received were easier to take than the ones in New Orleans because HOPE had the support of the city's political leaders.

Bolstered by public support, the Atlanta school board came up with a desegregation plan, as requested by the court, in December 1959.

Led by the mayor, Atlantans pressed the governor and the legislature for the right to decide for themselves whether to desegregate their schools, but Governor Vandiver reminded them of his campaign pledges and rejected their plea. Nevertheless, Atlantans were so persistent that the legislature created a school study commission to test public sentiment on desegregation. Atlanta was ready for this, and one of the city's leading business influentials—John Sibley, one of Vandiver's chief campaign contributors—became the head of the commission. The hearings surprised Governor Vandiver. In Atlanta, 85 of the 114 witnesses said they wanted the schools kept open. HOPE was so well organized that in five of the ten state districts which held hearings, a majority of witnesses spoke in favor of open schools and local initiative.

When Vandiver saw the strength of the open schools' forces, he relented and urged the legislature to repeal the school closing laws and to substitute laws that would permit local decisions. Outnumbered, Vandiver adopted Hartsfield's argument that school closings would blight the entire state. The legislature passed the substitute bills in January 1961.

The details of Atlanta's successful desegregation need not be set forth here. The two and a half years of political preparation resulted in a smooth operation. Nine carefully selected Negro high school seniors—all honor students and school leaders—entered four previously allwhite schools on August 30, 1961. Two of the schools were in well-to-do areas; two were in poor areas. Thus, no neighborhood or class could feel "picked on." Police permitted no loitering and arrested five persons who refused to move on. (Following their conviction, the five were all given jail sentences ranging from 30 to 60 days at hard labor.) White students interviewed in Atlanta by a New Orleans

*Times-Picayune* reporter said they wished people would "raise Cain like they did in New Orleans." But, unlike New Orleans, in Atlanta the decisions were made by the adults, not the teenagers.

In 1958 and 1959, Atlanta and New Orleans were confronted with similar problems. Both were in states that wanted to preserve segregation, but federal court orders requiring desegregation were likely to be issued before either state administration would have time or the money to create a "private" segregated school system. Without such a school system, massive state resistance to desegregation orders would probably mean that children would go without schools in New Orleans and Atlanta.

Both the governor of Georgia and the governor of Louisiana had come into office committed to preventing the federally ordered desegregation. Both had made the commitment in response to a challenge to their softness on segregation. Governor Vandiver of Georgia seemed even more committed than Louisiana's Governor Davis; Vandiver had even promised to prevent the desegregation with troops. But the prompt, unequivocal stand by Atlanta's political and business leaders in favor of peaceful desegregation persuaded Vandiver to back down and permit Atlanta to make its own decision. Atlanta's stand permitted .Vandiver to play the role of a statesman supporting home rule. As a result, Atlanta was able to control the desegregation process. Its reputation as a place to live and as a favorable place for business and industry was enhanced by the city's skilled handling of the situation.

By their passivity, New Orleans' business and political leaders left Governor Davis no alternative but to keep pressing his crusade against federal interference and racial mixing. They gave him no opportunity to be a statesman; they offered him no avenue for responsible retreat. Politically, neither governor could back down in the face of the federal government or the NAACP. Atlanta's leaders saw to it that Georgia's governor would not have to yield to the "enemy"; New Orleans' leaders enabled the governor to keep up his futile battle.

At the end of January 1961, after Davis's sales-tax proposal had been defeated in the Louisiana Senate, the *Times-Picayune* specialist on state politics observed that Davis had had a problem ever since the run-off, namely, how to "project an appearance of trying to prevent integration,. while faced with the apparent reality that nothing could be done to prevent it. . . . [His] problem has been made more troublesome by sporadic delusions that something could, indeed, be accomplished."[94] What fed these delusions? It seems clear now that it was the behavior of New Orleans' leaders. Virtually no one in New Orleans spoke for moderation except for a group of women who had absolutely no political influence in the state. Morrison, though Davis's natural enemy, exerted no pressure on Davis. The influential businessmen who tried to dissuade Davis from calling the special sessions did not want anyone to know they had done this. If no one in New Orleans cared enough to speak up for their city's school system, how could Davis go back on his promise to preserve segregation? He could have backed down only under some politically acceptable public pressure.

Davis needed visible pressure from moderate segregationists with political or economic power. The endorsement of moderate school board member Matthew Sutherland by the newspaper and the business leaders and the election of Sutherland came much too late to have any effect on Davis. The upstate legislators and Davis had already committed themselves. Had civic leaders been opposed to any threats to the public schools *from the very start,* as in Atlanta, the legislators and Davis might have found a way to make a "show" of opposing integration and the federal government while permitting New Orleans to go its own way if it chose to have integration. This would have been relatively easy since New Orleans was already considered "peculiar" in its racial attitudes.

But the absence of politics in New Orleans had greatly weakened the city. The resulting timidity of the city's mayor led in turn to the passivity of the business leaders. In the absence of local political leadership, control of desegregation was given over to the state legislature, the governor, and to private and semiprivate decision makers such as Leander Perez and the street mobs. Since reform had been one of the causes of the destruction of politics in New Orleans, it should not surprise us to learn that when an old-fashioned but modern politician like Victor Schiro became mayor, he was able to control desegregation and ensure that it would be accomplished peacefully. Like Schiro, Atlanta's Mayor Hartsfield was no race liberal, but he was a politician. Both mayors saw the *political* necessity for peaceful school desegregation.

# CHAPTER VII

## The Elite of New Orleans

Some observers place the blame for New Orleans' desegregation fiasco on the shoulders of the school board members, all five of whom were segregationists. Though this is only a surface reading of the situation, we should take a look at that surface. From 1956 to 1960, when they could have been preparing the public for desegregation, the board members were telling the public desegregation was not coming. Even after the school board knew that its efforts to defeat the desegregation suit had failed, this board continued to tell the people of New Orleans that they would never have to desegregate. If the board members did not know the day was coming, it could only be because they did not want to know. They hid from the facts for over four years.

The board's head-in-the-sands attitude undoubtedly contributed to the public's delusion: Only six months before the actual admission of Negroes to previously allwhite schools, desegregation must have seemed to most citizens of New Orleans to be either impossible or possible only in the remote future. If something is only remotely possible, one need not plan for it or even discuss it. The lack of public discussion of the issue kept the realities buried. The word of our respondents on this point is supported by Warren Breed's measurement of column inches on the issue in the *Times-Picayune*. In February 1960, there were *no* column inches devoted to the subject; in the first half of May, only 60 inches. But in the 15 days following Judge Wright's order of May 16, there were 320 inches, and the number increased thereafter.[95] In Atlanta, by contrast, the story was front page news as early as 1958. Unlike the sheltered New Orleanians, Atlantans had the opportunity to hear opposing points of view (and to learn thereby, incidentally, that a proponent of peaceful desegregation was not necessarily a Communist) and to learn what the alternatives were.

In November, after six months of vitriolic public discussion of the issue,

New Orleans school board member Matthew Sutherland ran on a save-the-schools platform and won. Of course, Sutherland was an incumbent, but it seems hard to believe that that would have helped him if the electorate were deeply committed to closing the schools. The point is that the vitriolic nature of the discussion did not hurt Sutherland. On the contrary, it had the effect of waking many of the voters to reality. Had the school board taken a stand earlier, the community would have had more time to make adjustments and build a save-the-schools movement. Even if the initial reaction to their position would have been hostile, an early stand by the board would have generated—early—the needed public discourse. Sutherland's campaign did accomplish this, but much too late.

Some observers have tried to make something of the board's racial ideology, but this proves to have been immaterial. On the civil rights scale of the National Opinion Research Center's questionnaire, the New Orleans school board members ranked sixth most conservative of the seven Southern school boards studied; only Montgomery's board ranked more conservative on race. Yet the conservative Montgomery school board had no difficulty achieving peaceful desegregation. In Montgomery, the elites came in, *uninvited,* to make sure desegregation went smoothly. It is clear, then, that the conservative racial ideology of the board was not the cause of New Orleans' difficulties.

The principal error that should be placed at the door of the school board was the decision to use the "computer" to select the schools to be integrated. The board knew it had other alternatives; it had been invited by two PTAs to send the Negro pupils to their schools. Yet these considerations were ignored by the board in its determination to make an objective, scientific decision. As we have seen, by ignoring political considerations, the board made the worst possible choice of schools.

But when one sees the whole situation, it becomes clear that the board can not be blamed for the city's fiasco. As we know, the board received very little help from other leaders in the community. The mayor did nothing; the elite did nothing; even the Girls were slow to organize. The save-the-schools campaign did not reach its peak (the testimonial dinner) until *after* the schools had already been damaged. The school board did make private overtures to all these people without success. What was being asked of the board was, after all, beyond it. It was being asked to make a decision for the entire community that would establish a major policy change. The school board lacked the power to do this by itself. It needed the legitimation of accepted leaders, but neither the mayor nor the city's elite would legitimate the board's attempts to achieve peaceful desegregation.

We know that the board's fundamental error in the selection of the schools was a natural consequence of the city's particular reform movement and the recruitment process. Determined to "take the school board out of politics," the reformers chose nonpolitical, "quality" candidates. In city after city, "quality" candidates turn out to be people who prefer a process of (middle class) adjustments instead of what they consider the (lower class) conflict inherent in politics. The board members proved to be true reform candidates, preferring "objective," "scientific," considerations to "subjective," political considerations.

Furthermore, by "removing the school board from politics," the reform isolated the board from sources of strength and support in the community. Since the board members were selected precisely because they had no political ties, it is not surprising that when they needed help they had no ties to sources of political power.

Because of the recruitment process and the criteria for recruitment, the men turned out to be honest but politically naive. Chosen because they were nonpolitical, they proved to be inexperienced at dealing with conflict. Unskilled at dealing with it, they were understandably frightened of conflict. Their reform orientation, lack of political confidence, and lack of political contacts led to their reliance on "objective" tests and contributed to their refusal to plan for desegregation.

What the board did turned out to be crucial *because* it was done in the absence of elites and in the absence of a political government. No matter what is said about the board, one still must ask why the elite and the political leaders did not act on their own and in their own interest to achieve peaceful desegregation. The Montgomery elite acted without any invitation. In Newark, to look at an "unreformed" Northern city for a moment, when the school board made an error and got embroiled in a battle with parents over the selection of schools to receive pupils from an overcrowded Negro school, the mayor told the school board to select different schools. It was to the political interest of the mayor that the schools be handled correctly. The New Orleans school board received no such helpful orders from its mayor.

The Montgomery economic elite not only entered the issue uninvited but stayed to direct the operation. Montgomery had two high schools, one attended chiefly by the "crackers," the other by the upper and middle class. The elite, sensing the trouble which would arise if only the "cracker" school were integrated, took the lead to ensure that both high schools would be integrated. As we know, the New Orleans school board chose its equivalent of the "cracker" schools, thus creating class conflict as well as sending

Negroes into the areas most hostile to them. Thus, the political leaders of Newark and the economic leaders of Montgomery played key roles either to prevent a mistake or to correct one already made. In New Orleans, the school board was left to make the decision by itself. When it made its political mistake, no one would accept responsibility for correcting it.

Thus, even when we try to explain the New Orleans story in terms of the omissions, errors, attitudes, and isolation of the school board, we still must come back to asking why the elite did not act on their own and in their own interest to achieve peaceful desegregation.

From a study of other Southern cities, we can see many steps that could have been taken to prevent the crisis or at least keep it to manageable proportions. The school board, the mayor, and the economic elite together could have appealed to several community values. At the minimum, they could have let the community know that they were opposed to demonstrations. The churches could have defined the demonstrations as un-Christian, and the businessmen could have warned—early and often—that disorder would prevent economic growth and reduce employment. The businessmen could have made it clear to Morrison that they would not tolerate street disturbances. In turn, Morrison could have had the police disperse the demonstrators and arrest those who resisted, and the local newspapers could have given the impression that those favoring violence were in the minority. In Atlanta and probably a hundred other Southern cities, these minimal steps were taken as a matter of course in preparing for integration. In New Orleans, because none of these steps was taken, those who favored moderation and keeping the schools open felt they were a beleaguered minority and were afraid to speak up when, as Sutherland's victory showed, they were actually in the majority.

Additionally, the elite (especially the *Times-Picayune*) could have been leaders of the save-the-schools movement. An advertising campaign could have been conducted. (Dallas businessmen, for example, bought space in streetcars.) Prominent backing could have been given to the two interfaith groups that had formed to stimulate discussion of the issues. As a further step, the top businessmen could have offered jobs and job security to parents like the Gabrielles to help them hold out. Such a gesture might have encouraged other parents to send their children back to school.

Above all, the elite could have advised the school board on the importance of choosing schools which would welcome token desegregation and could have assured the board of support if the board would begin the public discourse by taking an early stand.

Why the elite failed to act is, then, a critical question. The first and most obvious explanation for the failure of the elite to act was that perhaps there is no elite in New Orleans, that there is a power vacuum, that leadership is diffuse, fractionated, invisible, and therefore difficult or impossible to coordinate. But this was simply not so.

Two main approaches were taken to discover and identify the elite. The first was an analysis of the integration issue, in which we interviewed all five school board members, several of the more active Girls, members of CPE, civil rights leaders, aides and associates of Mayor Morrison, and individuals named by these people as community influentials. The people who were in the center of the events were asked to name the individuals whose support they had sought in order to legitimate the school board's token desegregation. We learned from them also which individuals had taken the key steps that finally ended the crisis.

The second approach was to ask our respondents the following two-part question:

> Suppose that there was a major program—something of great importance to this city. Which individual would be the one person who could be the most influential in getting the city to go through with the program? Who would be the other highly influential men who could help get it adopted?

One man was named by 20 of the 23 respondents who answered this question. Six of the 20 immediately named him as the most influential man in the city beyond a doubt. Another man was named by 11 of the 20 respondents, two were named seven times, and one was named six times. Regarding the man most frequently named, some of our respondents volunteered such comments as, "Everything has to be cleared with him." "His hand is behind everything that gets done in New Orleans." "No doors are closed to him." "If he's opposed to something, it can't get done."

A basic criticism of the reputational approach is that it reveals nothing more than a list of people with the reputation for influence and power. This approach, it is said, leads the researcher to focus on reputation rather than on behavior, that is, on "people who are *reputed* to be influential rather than on people who are *observed* to be influential."[96] Although this criticism ignores the fact that reputation for influence is at the very least one resource for power that a person may draw upon, the criticism is well taken. In this study, the researchers did not rely on reputation. The focus in this study was on behavior; reputation was used as one way of corroborating who the general influentials were. The striking fact was that the people whose names we obtained by studying behavior were the same people who ranked at the top of the reputational scale.

Looking at the history of the event that is the subject of this study, we saw that when the men who are on our list of key influentials would not endorse peaceful desegregation, the city was leaderless and decision making was chaotic. When these men backed peaceful desegregation, the city had peaceful desegregation. Apparently, their silence robbed the school board of the needed legitimacy in 1959 and 1960, and their participation in 1961 gave the school board legitimation.

The influence of these men is revealed in the history of other events as well. Public transportation was peacefully and smoothly desegregated in 1958. Like the school board, the governing body—New Orleans Public Service, Inc. (NOPSI)—fought desegregation as long as it could. But unlike the school board, NOPSI "prepared for the worst." Also unlike the school board, NOPSI is run by key community influentials—the same people who are on our list—and was able to use its power to make the desegregation possible.

In 1962, Negroes were threatening to hold public demonstrations because they were not allowed to sit on the benches in the city park. Mayor Schiro refused to meet with the Negroes because he had a meeting to attend. But the man who ranked as our number one influential persuaded the mayor to leave his meeting and to meet instead with the Negroes. The demonstrations were averted.

These men have negative power, too. In 1962, 1963, and 1964, extensive efforts were made by Negro leaders and some members of the elite to get the mayor to appoint a biracial committee to handle racial problems. Many moderates backed this proposal, and the Mayor let it be known that he favored such a committee. But because two of the top men on our list, including the number one man, opposed the formation of such a committee, no such committee was formed.

Thus, not only do the men on our list have the reputation for being influential, but they also hold positions of authority and influence, and when they want the mayor to do something, he does it; when they oppose something the mayor is supporting, it does not get done.

One more point needs to be made in this connection. The elite of New Orleans not only know each other, but they are also good friends, belong to the same clubs, check with one another on the telephone, and even write to one another on civic issues. They prefer to act (or not act) in concert. (But they do not meet regularly, formally, or systematically, as do their counterparts in Dallas, for example.) So it is definitely not true that the New Orleans elite is diffuse, fractionated, or unable to coordinate its efforts.

## THE ELITE: "GOOD BREEDING" VS. "GOOD BUSINESS"

Is there some characteristic of the New Orleans elite, then, that will help to explain their failure to act in such a major community decision? The answer is yes: They are a traditionalist, nonmodernizing elite. Six members of the elite—including three of the four men most frequently named as influentials—were asked how long they had lived in New Orleans and how they felt about the city. All but one was born in New Orleans. Four of the six volunteered the information that their family had been in New Orleans for over a century, and two of the four noted that their family had been in Louisiana for over one hundred fifty years.

Two other members of the elite were so young that the interviewer asked how they had risen to positions of key influence so rapidly. They answered, in effect, that they had not "risen"; they had entered automatically because they were the sons of influential men in New Orleans. "My influence," said one, "is chiefly inheritance and elbow grease." The other identified his father and concluded, "I knew the elite socially and was in automatically."

When asked about their attachment to New Orleans, the elite seemed to be describing not a city but a country club. "Ideal social atmosphere. Relaxed, pleasant living." "The way of life." "Pleasant and gracious." "Most wonderful atmosphere. Finest fishing in the world. Pace is good. Beautiful spring and fall. Every sport but hockey."

To these comments, two of the top three men added (and emphasized) that, "The dollar sign means little in New Orleans." "A man without money can have anything the city has to offer. Without money a girl in New Orleans can have a debut. In Houston, it costs $10,000 to join the 'good' country clubs. Here there is no wealthy clique."

Putting together the extent to which the elite are natives of New Orleans and the comments about money being unimportant, we get a picture of a society in which wealth is indeed unimportant. Family and inheritance—sometimes called "good breeding" in the South—and place of birth count for everything. It is true that the girl without money can have a debut, but not any girl—only the girl from the "right" family. This has two social consequences: A person from a "good" family stays in the elite no matter how far his financial status declines—a former king of the Mardi Gras remains socially prominent even though he has had to turn his home into a boarding house;

secondly, a new person, no matter what he has made of himself and how much wealth he has amassed, finds it difficult to crash the inner circle. Wealth is not convertible into social standing. Achieved status is irrelevant; family background is the chief determinant of status.

The result is a (relatively) closed elite, and a closed elite is a stagnant elite, unrefreshed by new blood and new attitudes. It is impossible to discuss New Orleans in this connection without immediately thinking of two sharp contrasts—Atlanta and, since the New Orleans elite raised it, Houston. Houston and Atlanta are attracting both people and industry, some of the latter from the New Orleans area.

In Houston and Atlanta, wealth is easily converted into social standing. The result in both cities is an open elite. All one needs is the money to join the good club. Consequently, a person can fall from the elite if he fails to "keep up" with the others, and a new person from another city can easily crash the elite. The elite is thus constantly refreshed by new blood and new attitudes.

When the interviewer, in talking to members of the New Orleans elite, referred to Atlanta or Houston, the response was invariably one of disdain: "Who would want to live *there?*" The New Orleans elite characterized Houston and Atlanta as brash, money-grubbing, repugnant cities run by the *nouveau riche,* lacking in culture and civility, caught in the spirit of vulgar boosterism. Further, the two rival cities were considered by the New Orleans elite not to be truly Southern cities.

Since money is not a determinant of status in New Orleans, it is not surprising to learn that the New Orleans elite is not engaged in a single-minded pursuit of wealth and business interests. The status of the elites is so secure that they feel no need to drive themselves or hustle to maintain their position. Their attitude was candidly reflected in a *Times-Picayune* editorial in January 1961. The editorial dealt with the question of what was unique about New Orleans, and the writer noted that differences between cities have been greatly reduced—skyscrapers, supermarkets, and cloverleaf exchanges look the same all over. The French Quarter, of course, was unique.

> But aside from this, it might be argued that mostly what remains of New Orleans' distinctiveness is a state of mind. For it takes a certain attitude toward life and work and fun to turn out a goodly part of the town for a parade on any pretext, to keep a luncheon club member at the rummy table while a client waits at the office. . . .[97]

One cannot picture the typical businessmen of Atlanta or Houston keeping a client waiting at the office while they play games at the club. In 1962,

Atlanta's Mayor Ivan Allen, Jr., characterized his city in this way: "This is not a playboy's town, and it's not a cocktail-at-lunch town. This is a businessman's town."[98] The playboy's town could very well be the city where the clients are kept waiting while the businessmen are at the club. *Because* the New Orleans elite are not so concerned about their business interests, they find it difficult to get exercised about the economic development of the city.*

There are some men in New Orleans now who are busily engaged in booster-type activity. Some of these men are New Yorkers making New Orleans a second home and some are native New Orleanians with socially unacceptable family backgrounds. The elite spoke with great contempt for these "promoters" and "outsiders."**

Repeatedly, the New Orleans elite blamed all their troubles on "outsiders." This hostility to outsiders breeds a lack of sensitivity to the beliefs and attitudes and concerns of outsiders. This goes a great way toward explaining why the New Orleans elite did not concern itself with the effect its city's chaotic desegregation was having on the rest of the nation's attitude toward New Orleans.

* The following description of New Orleans in the early nineteenth century indicates that this distinctive state of mind has had a long history in New Orleans.

> Lloyd's of London is said to have prophesied in 1821 that New Orleans would become the greatest port in the world. . . . Certainly the makings of the world's busiest port were there. Even the ocean-going vessels of today can unload from their holds right into the warehouses on the levees, with no cartage at all. But in 1821 and for several years after, New Orleans had no warehouses on the levees and few anywhere in the city. She had not troubled to build so much as a roof over her wharves. Cargoes stood out on the levees in all sorts of weather. The losses of perishables were on a scale a Boston merchant would have called criminal—$100,000 in tobacco in one season. Flour and pork went moldy; hides dried out. The Orleanians shrugged, laughed, said easily that if insurance did not cover the loss, another shipment and another deal would. Until 1833, the city had no central market, no public warehouses, no auction rooms, no exchange. A captain landing an unconsigned shipment had himself to scurry around to find a buyer. Men conducted their business on a personal basis, frequently in one of the wine shops or restaurants. There was neither business organization nor wish for it. Life was gay, easy, leisurely. Citizens let themselves believe that the city's position made her forever immune to attack from competitors. . . . New Orleans . . . remained unconcerned until it was too late.
> —Constance McLaughlin Green, *American Cities* (Tuckahoe, N. Y.: De Graff, 1957), pp. 72-73.

** New Orleans' boosters played no role in the 1960 desegregation crisis. Excluded from the elite, lacking influence with Chep Morrison, they not only had no base from which to exert influence, but they were neither asked nor expected to play a role. The new mayor, however, has been much more receptive to these men, and they are beginning to exert some influence, particularly with regard to urban renewal and the attraction of new industry.

The outsider is not only welcome in Atlanta and Houston, he is eagerly sought after. Since Atlanta's leaders are chiefly concerned with achieved status and wealth, they are eager to attract Northern money. Eager to attract new money and new people, Atlanta's leaders are very sensitive to the effects local conditions have on the attitudes of outsiders toward their city. The slogan of Atlanta's leaders—"We are too busy to hate"—means that racial strife hurts business. Consequently, even though Atlanta's leaders may have anti-Negro feelings, they try not to let those feelings interfere with their goal of enriching themselves by attracting more money to their city. It was only natural, then, for Atlanta's leaders to see immediately the necessity for achieving peaceful desegregation.

Being traditionalist, the New Orleans elite carries the traditional prejudice of the region. Being largely closed to Northerners, New Orleans' elite society is a Southern group, and an old Southern group at that. ("My grandfather fought in the Confederate Army.") It is a group with strong anti-Negro feelings or at least a strong aversion to changing the traditional pattern of relationships between Negro and white. This, too, helps to explain the reluctance to aid in the desegregation of the schools. In this connection, the reader should recall that the *Times-Picayune* (whose publisher and editor were named as influentials) had great difficulty deciding which would be a greater disaster, integration or closing the schools. The reader should recall also that one of the key elites conditioned his support for the school board on the segregation of toilets in the elementary schools.

In contrast, the Atlanta elite, by being open, has drawn into its circle many Northerners and other businessmen not bound by the traditional prejudices of the South. The result is that the Atlanta elite is not deeply troubled by events that break the traditional relationships between the races—or at least is not willing to let these feelings determine its public attitude. In New Orleans, the white leaders who now meet with Negro leaders to iron out problems do so only in secret and refuse to form a biracial committee. In Atlanta, communication between leaders of the two races is frequently considered the best in the South. The Atlanta elite are not ashamed to be seen meeting with Negro leaders.

## THE POLITICAL CONSEQUENCES

What are the political consequences for a city with a traditionalist elite as that of New Orleans? One is that the mayor—even a "reform" mayor—is less likely to move into controversial areas or take steps that will draw outsiders to the city. In Atlanta's more open society, the mayor is more likely to take such steps. The New Orleans mayor has little impetus to do so; the Atlanta mayor knows he is expected to be a booster. Even though Atlanta's Mayor Hartsfield acted *before* the business elite did in working for peaceful deseg-regation, he felt he could count on their support. And they did support him.

But the essential political consequence of a closed, traditionalist elite is that the elites have no political interest. Being withdrawn from politics and lacking interest in the economic development of the city, the New Orleans elite do not go out and elect their own mayor. The Atlanta elite make sure they get a mayor who has the businessmen's welfare at heart. They are proud to be deeply involved in this process. To them, civic leadership is a further mark of distinction. This attitude has provided Atlanta with two outstand-ing, vigorous mayors—both of them prominent businessmen—who boost the city and work assiduously to attract new wealth to it. In the same period, New Orleans had first a corrupt, illiterate mayor (Maestri) with ties to the underworld and then a playboy mayor (Morrison) who spent much of his time cultivating a state constituency for his gubernatorial ambitions. Each group of elites got the government it wanted and deserved. When New Orleans was close to mob rule, its mayor was blaming the trouble on—that's right—"outsiders." After first blaming Leander Perez, then Jimmie Davis, then the federal government, Morrison settled on the "real" culprit—the outside press. Atlanta's mayor made sure there was no trouble and then invited the world's press to come and observe how progressive and civilized Atlanta was. He even took the reporters on a tour of the city's Negro section.

The two cities, of course, differ from one another in many respects. One difference worth noting here is in the relationship of the city to its state. Because of the gross malapportionment of the Georgia legislature, Atlanta's mayors are rarely involved in state politics; likewise, the Georgia governor has little need to forge alliances with the city politicians. Mayor Hartsfield always said he was much too busy running his city to be pursuing other interests.

New Orleans' mayor not only has a lot more spare time, but he also has much reason to be involved in state politics. New Orleans has long been fairly represented in both the state legislature and the state's Central Democratic Committee. And, as we have noted, the state constitution forces New Orleans mayors to build alliances with the state administration and encourages Louisiana governors to interfere in city politics.

In addition, there were the personal idiosyncrasies of Chep Morrison, not the least of which was his pursuit of the governor's office. Though no Catholic and no New Orleans mayor had ever been elected governor in that Protestant, rural, Catholic-hating state, Catholic Chep Morrison kept trying even though his candidacy suffered the further disability of his having the reputation as a racial progressive. Thus, he was bent on creating a state constituency in a state which was opposed to the programs his principal local supporters most wanted. Whatever he did that was good for New Orleans hurt him with his state constituency; whatever helped him with his state constituency, hurt his city.*

Yet, idiosyncratic as Morrison's behavior was, one must still look to the elite attitude. Had the New Orleans elite been more active and interested in politics, they would have recruited a man who would not have behaved as he did. In Atlanta, the business elite tried to find candidates amenable to their interests; in New Orleans, the elite withdrawal permitted the recruitment of a young man who had "never met a payroll," a dabbler in politics who was chosen for his war record, his looks, and his availability. No one else wanted to run, least of all the businessmen. If the elite never run for office and do not want to participate in politics, it follows that the man who does run is never a member of the elite and, more importantly, can not count on the support of the elite for his policies and actions. The elite withdrawal made it possible for a loner like Morrison to become the mayor. When the controls are off, the field is open to idiosyncratic personalities.

"We were the first in the Deep South, so how could we prepare for it?" In slightly altered form, this question was raised in defense of the city's behavior by several New Orleanians. But New Orleans' elite had refused to learn from the mistakes and solutions of other Southern cities—notably Little Rock. One must recall that a businessman from Little Rock went to New Orleans to warn the city's economic leaders that failure to achieve peaceful desegregation could hurt the city financially, but his advice was ignored. In Atlanta, on the other hand, the mayor had a study of Little Rock prepared and distributed to the city's elite.

Furthermore, Atlanta's elite had already been preparing for the desegregation for two years when New Orleans' schools were desegregated. Thus, those who say Atlanta had the opportunity to learn from New Orleans' mistakes miss the point. Atlanta learned from Little Rock's mistakes and set to work

* As a New Orleans newspaperman explained, in evaluating Morrison's chance to be elected governor in 1960, "The kind of mayor who looks right taking Zsa Zsa Gabor to tea looks all wrong to those rednecks up in the hill parishes." Quoted in A. J. Liebling, *The Earl of Louisiana* (New York: Simon and Schuster, 1961), p. 45.

immediately to avoid them. New Orleans could have learned from Little Rock's mistakes *and* Atlanta's two years of careful preparation, but chose not to.

Additionally, one wonders whether some of these things had to be "learned." Did New Orleans really need the example of another city to know not to let a mob crowd around a mother and her child for two months? It is standard police procedure to keep crowds away if no trouble is wanted. An Atlanta leader was surprised to hear praise for Atlanta's smooth desegregation. "If we had not done this in the right way," he explained, "we would have been the stupidest people in the world."[99] Still, it can not be said that New Orleans' leaders were stupid. Their failure to learn was a *refusal* to learn.

What emerges, then, is a city with a powerful elite that is reluctant to participate in local political affairs. It is a highly traditionalist elite, chiefly concerned with "good breeding" and the exclusiveness of aristocratic association. It is primarily native-born, with inheritance being the chief determinant of social position. Since the elite is a closed one and since it is a traditionalist elite, the city does not have a "climate of progress" to give impetus to programs and policies that attract people and industry.

Given sufficient pressure, Chep Morrison might have been willing to lead the city to peaceful desegregation of the schools, but there was no spirit of "getting the city moving" either to encourage him or to reward him if he took the necessary steps. The "spirit of progress" in Atlanta not only tells the mayor what is expected of him but rewards him with great local prestige. When the crisis loomed and then hit New Orleans as friends had warned it would, the elite—secure in its status and uninterested in economic progress— refused to support the mayor, the school board, or the Girls, and by so refusing, denied legitimation to the moderate efforts of the school board. When a group as powerful as the New Orleans elite refuses to sanction a controversial program, it ensures the failure of that program.

It is essential to note that whereas New Orleans' Morrison had the reputation, at least, as a liberal on race matters, Atlanta's Hartsfield was definitely *not* a liberal on race matters. Yet, because Atlanta's elite is concerned with the economic development of the city and with the attraction of new wealth, and because the elite is interested in playing a political role, Atlanta's mayor took the lead in peaceful school desegregation.*

* Four years later, Edward Banfield noted the same thing. "On the race issue most of [Atlanta's] big businessmen are personally far from liberal. However, they have been persuaded by the newspapers and the politicians that desegregation is inevitable and efforts to delay it will only harm the city's 'image.' When Mayor Allen returned to Atlanta after tes-

## TRANSITION TO BOOSTERISM?

By finally forcing the elite to play a public role, the crisis of 1960 may prove to have been a turning point in the attitude and behavior of the New Orleans elite. Their old patterns and relationships were broken and proved insufficient. Jarred from their security, they have learned that they must participate more actively in political affairs. In addition, they have come to realize the limitations of their super-cautious Chamber of Commerce (which simply tables every resolution dealing with race) and have attempted to bypass it with an organization named the Committee for a Better Louisiana (CABL) which is working to attract industry to the state. They know now that industry is restrained from moving to Louisiana, in part, by the image of bad politics in the state, and they now realize they must do something to overcome this image. This first step, limited as it is, involves drastic changes in the attitudes of the elite.

Ever since the 1960 school crisis and the subsequent demise of the Morrison regime, a new breed of businessmen have been on the rise in the city. These men are boosters and promoters, and, as mentioned previously, they are much despised by the established elite. These "brash" men fit in very well with the new mayor, Victor Schiro, who appears to be more of a businessman's mayor than Morrison. Schiro's approach, as we have seen, has already improved the image of the city, and the boosterism of the new businessmen is second to none. On the other hand, there are some ironic aspects to the progress of New Orleans' boosters. Their crowning success thus far has been the obtainment of a lucrative franchise for a professional football team. But the promoter who played the leading role in getting the franchise is a transplanted New Yorker, the dominant political role has been played by the state's governor rather than the mayor, and the money for the team comes from a combine led by a Houston oil man. Another achievement of the boosters—a 45-story building that was to be a showcase for the new spirit of the city—ran into serious trouble. Sam Recile, the realtor behind this project, had to file bankruptcy

---

tifying in favor of the federal civil rights bill, he found that his fellow businessmen all opposed the stand he had taken. They were so 'hot after my skin,' he said afterward, that he got Ralph McGill of the *Constitution* to talk to some of them. Later the Chamber of Commerce's magazine, reporting on the mayor's trip to Washington, said, 'Certainly the Forward Atlanta advertising kitty [a fund raised by the Chamber to boost the city] couldn't have bought the round of praise Allen earned for Atlanta, from Congress to the editorial pages of the *New York Times*. The wire services built it into the biggest Atlanta-image impact since the city peacefully desegregated its schools.' " Edward C. Banfield, *Big City Politics* (New York: Random House, 1965), p. 31.

to protect his company from its many creditors, with the result that the building may be forced to be auctioned even before its completion. Meanwhile, rumors of scandals involving the mayor's office and land speculation float through the city.

It is not easy to see the direction New Orleans will take in the next 25 years. If the promoters overextend themselves, as Recile did, and if the mayor's office is touched by scandal, a new wave of reform could sweep the city. If, by that time, the old elite have not fully entered public life, reform could give the city another Chep Morrison. On the other hand, if the elite enter public life and exert their influence, they could bring a new way of life to New Orleans.

# CHAPTER VIII

## Politics and Reality

In the absence of the elites, where was everyone else? The problem was not that the message did not get through to the elites, but that there was no one to give them the message.

The behavior of the New Orleans elite has its roots in what many have called the "rape" of the city in the 1930s, but which, on closer look, was an emasculation. The women are politically effective; the men seem to have lost their vigor. To summarize very briefly, the Longs destroyed the fiscal solvency of New Orleans, forced its mayor to resign in midterm, installed a hand-picked man in the office, and eliminated the next election date. In 1940, with the city in the grip of its political enemies, the city delivered a majority of its vote for the enemy—Earl Long—even though the Longs had been waging open war on the city for the previous ten years. To add to the irony, the Long faction had just been caught in some of the most colossal scandals ever seen in the United States, and many of its members were sent to the penitentiary. The scandals were so outrageous that the rest of the state had defeated Earl Long.

Though Louisiana is a one-party state, it has enjoyed a reatively stable bifactionalism within this system.[100] But from the mid-1930s on, following the "rape," no bifactionalism was in evidence in New Orleans. As we have seen, the city's capitalists have at times even backed the agrarian welfare-state Long faction. One recalls in this connection that the city's leading anti-Longs praised anti-Long Mayor Walmsley for resigning, were publicly grateful for Longite Governor Leche's "generosity" in restoring to the city fiscal powers he had taken away from it, and raised no outcry against the conquest of their city by the Long machine. Later, many businessmen refused to back Morrison in his campaign to unseat Maestri. And the leaders in the move to close the schools in 1960—Governor Davis and State Superintendent of Education

Shelby Jackson—were in the anti-Long faction, the supposedly "good govern-ment" faction. The conservative businessmen of New Orleans and even some leading racial moderates had supported Davis in his election campaign.

It would be difficult to conceive of a less secure political structure in an American city than the one that existed in New Orleans. It was built on the uncertainly shifting sands of the Long- anti-Long bifactionalism, periodically shaken by state buccaneering against the city, and rent internally by many factors, most notably the lone wolf politics of Chep Morrison and the reform movement, which cut across party and factional lines. The internal divisions prevented the city even from having a unified response to the state attacks against the city. And all this political confusion, of course, was embedded in the nondemocratic context of a one-party system. Conservative New Orleans businessmen who supported Nixon in 1960 and Goldwater in 1964 told the author of this book that they were Democrats. (They were not lying or joking. One *has* to be a Democrat in Louisiana.) Furthermore, since the primary determines the outcome of most elections, the ballot contains neither party names nor symbols to guide the voters. The confusion, the lack of cohesion among the anti-Longs, the lack of clear factional lines—all these left New Orleans with a politics so pulverized that it became easy for leaders to avoid taking a stand on issues. Those who take part in civic affairs in New Orleans are rarely sure who is on their side, whom to trust, or whom to turn to for help. Even the Girls have frequent internal conflicts and are never quite sure who their true friends are within the movement.

In this political environment, politics is an even more dangerous and am-biguous undertaking than it is in other big cities. These conditions reinforced the nonpolitical impulses of the elite. If any of the elite had wanted to enter public life, one look would have told them it was much safer to stick to the pleasures of the clubs and to pretend not to know or care about local politics. In such a political environment, it is not surprising that the elite shrank from the intensely emotional issue of school integration. In such an environment, it is understandable that a group of women would seek, in motherly fashion, to protect and isolate the schools from the evil and confusing political world. Not knowing whom to trust, not knowing which faction could help—the anti-Longs were the "good government" faction which cared little about schools; the Longs were the "corrupt machine politicians" who traditionally used New Orleans as a whipping boy—the women naturally sought to create their own faction.

## THE NONPOLITICS OF REFORM

Yet the difficulties were exacerbated by the long-run effects of the reform movement. The problems which called the reform movement into existence were real and pressing—the corruption, the abuse of patronage, and the decline of the school system were intolerable. But the mere removal of corrupt politics is not enough. It must be replaced by something which can at least cope with the problems corruption was coping with. Despite the undoubted good accomplished by New Orleans' reform movement in ridding the school system of corruption, the movement introduced an unrealistic attitude typical of reform movements everywhere.

Politicians, even corrupt ones, as politicians at least know that different people have different interests and that the normal state of these different interests is to be in constant conflict. Like other reformers both before and after them in many cities, the Girls think that man's political problems can be solved by "scientific administration," finding the one "best" solution. This is what the reform school board members were doing when they used objective tests to determine which schools to integrate. The Girls, like other reformers, were interested, as E. L. Woodward said of Bentham, "not in the problems of life, but in the mechanism of living."[101] Thus the Girls decided to reform the schools by "taking them out of politics." But with their narrow view of politics—to them, as to reformers everywhere, it means little more than corruption and a pigheaded use of patronage—taking the schools out of politics meant taking the schools out of the realm where the problems of life are dealt with. By viewing politics so narrowly, the reformers saw the remedy only in terms of changing the *structure* rather than in terms of changing the *policy* of the school system. Thus, civil service was substituted for patronage and the school board members were recruited for their honesty, independence, and interest in the schools, *but they were not questioned in advance about their views on matters of policy.* One of the men they recruited in this fashion (and elected to the school board) turned out to be all they had asked for: He was, indeed, honest, independent, and interested in the schools. But he was also an organizer of the White Citizens' Council. We see here the full implications and consequences of the Girls' attitude toward politics. They were so singlemindedly concerned about structure, about honesty in government, that they neglected the much more vital questions about what the policy of the school system should be. When the world began to crumble around the school system, there was one of the honest, independent, reform school board members working to close down the schools to avoid integration.

Furthermore, by placing such a high value on independence from politics,

the Girls recruited men who were isolated from sources of strength and unskilled at creating public support. It should be no surprise that the politically
naïve board members would shrink from the school integration issue and
pretend that integration was not imminent. They had no one to turn to for
help and advice, and, being reformed, they had no political boss to give them
orders. (The Democratic mayor—unsurprisingly, in this environment, a lone
wolf—disliked controversy so intensely that he made a point of being neutral
in the presidential elections of both 1948 and 1952. Besides, the mayor needed
the support of the New Orleans-hating, die-hard segregationists in the rest
of the state for his gubernatorial campaigns.) It is understandable, then, that
when the issue was forced upon them, these school board members at first
sought refuge in "objective tests" instead of looking for a political solution
for their problems.

This is not the place to discuss the source of the reform view of politics, but
it is worth noting that it is a middle class view of the world. The vision is that
conflict is an evil that can be eliminated by "correct" decisions arrived at by
"good" people without the use of power. The reformers' vision of the world
is a place where nice, intelligent, rational people who are all in agreement
with one another sit around and make rational decisions. But this vision is
a pure fantasy, for not even the middle class is at peace with itself, and only
a small amount of conflict in the world is between "bad" people and "good"
people.

## THE VALUE OF POLITICS

People crave a government—even in New Orleans. Decisions must be made.
Problems must be dealt with. Conflicts must be adjusted, accommodated, and
compromised. A political government allows for the interplay of conflicting
interests within a safe context. All this was missing in New Orleans.

A political government provides something else that was missing in New
Orleans—a public forum for the testing out and the playing out of ideas and
viewpoints and positions and leaders. I have made much of the removal of
the school board from politics, but from another point of view what politics
was there to remove them from? Similarly, I have made much of the withdrawal by the elite into private life and the pleasures of their clubs. But in
New Orleans where else could they be? There was no public forum, no
public space, no politics to participate in.

Historically, the withdrawal of New Orleans' elite preceded the destruction
of politics. For a time—the late 1920s and early 1930s—these were parallel

developments. But starting with the mid-30s the two developments began acting upon each other as interconnecting causes, reinforcing one another, and deepening the effects of one another. It is not possible to say that one is the cause and the other the effect. Still, it is possible to conclude that if the city had had a political government the absence of the elites would not have mattered as much as it did.

That people crave a government in New Orleans was evident during the city's crisis. When Morrison, the elite, and, to a lesser extent, the Catholic hierarchy failed to play a political role, the people did not become anarchic. They turned to other leaders, such as Perez and certain members of the legislature. That there was a certain amount of anarchy can be attributed in large part to a strategy of anarchy, e.g., the wild demonstrations at the schools and the raids on peoples' homes. But the chief cause of the chaos lay in the limited means available to Perez and the legislators to govern New Orleans. Furthermore, Perez and the state legislators could play only a partisan role; they could not accommodate conflicting viewpoints.

As we have seen, the four board members who tried to keep the schools open were virtually without influence with Morrison, the elite, and the state government. Yet gradually these four men and others allied with them learned to play politics. Eventually, they even created a sub elite. ("Sub" in two senses: under or lesser than the city's true elite, and as a substitute for them.) The board members and their allies found a number of people with some standing in the community and helped them form the organization known as the Committee for Public Education (CPE). Then the CPE, by means of the *Williams* case, helped Judge Wright "force" the school board to integrate. This is skillful politics. Yet it was learned at great cost to the city. Had the city's politics not been pulverized by the cumulative effects of the Longs, the Morrison regime, and the concerns of the reformers, the job of mobilizing support and useful pressures could have been accomplished more quickly and with considerably more ease—and the city could have been spared a great deal of pain.

With the exception of Judge Skelly Wright, virtually every important person discussed in this study hid from the realities of the city's situation. The school board pretended integration was not coming; the elite told themselves that what happened did not matter or at least could not affect them; Morrison thought he could retain his position by remaining neutral just one more time; Davis thought he really could prevent integration; and, much earlier, the Girls thought they could save the schools without facing the problems of life that are encountered in running a school system. Had politics not been pulverized in the city, this mass escape from reality would not have been possible. The pulverization of politics permitted men in New Orleans to feel free of the political pressures which men in countless other Southern cities felt and responded to.

The failure of the parochial system to desegregate, the presence of Leander Perez, the fact that New Orleans was the first big city in the Deep South to integrate its schools, and the fact that the conflict over the schools was the city's first serious racial trouble—these factors (and many others) were raised by New Orleanians as excuses for their city's social breakdown in 1960. These may have been contributing factors, but the basic cause of this social breakdown was the city's *political* breakdown. Though the city's political breakdown was, as we have seen, of long standing, the breakdown had been concealed, in part, by the economic boom enjoyed by the city during World War II but mainly by the carefree attitude and lack of civic consciousness on the part of the elite. The concealment failed when the city was faced with the crisis over the schools. Enlightened New Orleanians blame the troubles of 1960 on the abdication of responsibility by the elite. But it was the disorganization and pulverization of politics that kept the city dependent upon its traditionalist elite. To deal with change, to cope with reality, *any* community needs political organization.

There are many meanings to this story, but probably the one that has the widest relevance is that we cannot come to grips with the problems of our social life without organizing to build constituencies, without mobilizing and utilizing community support, without, in short, making use of political power. Above all, these problems cannot be dealt with by technical expertise, by exclusive concern for efficient mechanisms, or by scientific administration. The *policies* of our institutions, not the honesty of the men who govern them, must be our primary concern. Thus, if we are to reform our school systems, we must be concerned with policy questions: Whom shall we educate? What shall we educate them for? What do we want them to know? Reformers have traditionally concerned themselves with the questions of civil service, the merit system, honesty in government, and the independence of school board members from politics. But these technical matters are not only less important than policy issues, but, as we have seen with the case of New Orleans, an exclusive concern with them can be destructive of the very institution reform was intended to save. In this sense, this study is not about school integration or about New Orleans but about the need for reformers (and others who wish to improve our life) to quit tinkering with technical matters and to concentrate instead on the substance of policy.

# Footnotes

1. The cities are San Francisco, St. Louis, Pittsburgh, Buffalo, Newark, Baltimore, Jacksonville, Miami, Atlanta, Montgomery, Columbus (Georgia), Baton Rouge, New Orleans, and two Northern cities which I cannot name because of promises of anonymity. See Robert L. Crain, Morton Inger, James Vanecko, and Gerald McWorter, *The Politics of School Desegregation* (Chicago: Aldine, 1968).
2. This definition is drawn from Harold D. Lasswell, Daniel Lerner, and C. Easton Rothwell, *The Comparative Study of Elites* (Hoover Institute Studies, Series B: "Elites," No. 1; Stanford, California: Stanford University Press, 1952), p. 6.
3. Helen Fuller, "New Orleans Knows Better," *New Republic*, February 16, 1959, p. 16.
4. *Ibid.*
5. Allan P. Sindler, *Huey Long's Louisiana* (Baltimore: Johns Hopkins Press, 1956), p. 198.
6. Seymour Freedgood, "New Strength in City Hall," *Fortune*, November 1957, p. 157.
7. *New York Times*, May 8, 1960, p. 67.
8. Ralph G. Martin, "New Orleans Has Its Face Lifted," *New Republic*, June 2, 1947, p. 19.
9. All figures in this paragraph are from L. Vaughan Howard and Robert S. Friedman, *Government in Metropolitan New Orleans* ("Tulane Studies in Political Science," Vol. VI; New Orleans: Tulane University Press, 1959), p. 119.
10. *Brown v. Board of Education of Topeka*, 349 U.S. 294 (1955).
11. *Bush v. Orleans Parish School Board*, 138 F. Supp. 337, 342 (1956).
12. Louisa Dolcher, "A Time of Worry in 'The City Care Forgot,'" *Reporter*, March 8, 1956, p. 17.
13. *Orleans Parish School Board v. Bush*, 242 F. 2nd 156 (affirmed, March 1, 1957); 354 U.S. 921 (cert. denied, June 17, 1957); 252 F. 2nd 253 (affirmed, Feb. 13, 1958); 356 U.S. 969 (cert. denied, May 26, 1958).
14. *Orleans Parish School Board v. Bush*, United States District Court, Eastern District, Louisiana, Civil Action No. 3630, *Race Relations Law Reporter*, IV (Nashville: Vanderbilt University School of Law, 1959), 583.
15. *New York Times*, May 8, 1960, p. 67.
16. *Bush v. Orleans Parish School Board*, United States District Court, Eastern District, Louisiana, Civil Action No. 3630, *Race Relations Law Reporter*, V (Nashville: Vanderbilt University School of Law, 1960), 378.
17. A. J. Liebling, *The Earl of Louisiana* (New York: Simon and Schuster, 1961), p. 46.
18. *Ibid.*, p. 197.
19. *State of Louisiana v. Orleans Parish School Board*, 118 So. 2nd 471 (1960).
20. William Peters, *The Southern Temper* (Garden City, N.Y.: Doubleday, 1959), p. 106.

21. *Newsweek,* March 5, 1956, p. 51.

22. *New York Times,* July 8, 1959, p. 20.

23. *New Orleans Times-Picayune,* June 26, 1960, sec. 2, p. 2. Hereinafter referred to as the *Times-Picayune.*

24. Warren Breed, "The Emergence of Pluralistic Public Opinion in a Community Crisis," *Applied Sociology,* Alvin W. Gouldner and S. M. Miller, eds. (New York: Free Press of Glencoe, 1965), p. 136.

25. *State of Louisiana v. Orleans Parish School Board,* Civil District Court for Parish of Orleans, *Race Relations Law Reporter,* V (Nashville: Vanderbilt University School of Law 1960), 659.

26. *New York Times,* August 14, 1960, p. 56.

27. *Times-Picayune,* August 21, 1960, p. 16.

28. *New York Times,* August 14, 1960, p. 56.

29. *Bush v. Orleans Parish School Board; Williams v. Davis,* 187 F. Supp. 42 (1960).

30. *Ibid.,* United States District Court, Eastern District, La., *Race Relations Law Reporter,* V (Nashville: Vanderbilt University School of Law, 1960), 669; motion to vacate denied, 364 U.S. 803 (1960).

31. See H. W. Gilmore, "The Old New Orleans and the New: A Case for Ecology," *Sociology and History,* Werner J. Cahnman and Alvin Boskoff, eds. (New York: Free Press of Glencoe, 1964), pp. 422–34.

32. Calvin Trillin, "The Zulus," *New Yorker,* June 20, 1964, p. 68.

33. Testimony of Mrs. Mary Sand, president of SOS, Inc., United States Commission on Civil Rights, *Third Annual Conference on Problems of Schools in Transition: From the Educator's Viewpoint* (Williamsburg, Va., 1961), p. 53.

34. *Times-Picayune,* November 2, 1960, p. 10.

35. *Ibid.,* November 5, 1960, p. 5.

36. *Ibid.,* p. 19.

37. *Ibid.,* November 4, 1960, sec. 2, p. 7.

38. *Ibid.,* November 6, 1960, p. 21.

39. *Ibid.,* November 5, 1960, p. 19.

40. *Bush v. Orleans Parish School Board; Williams v. Davis; United States v. Louisiana,* 188 F. Supp. 916, 928 (November 30, 1960).

41. *Times-Picayune,* November 5, 1960, p. 19.

42. *Ibid.*

43. Figures from *ibid.,* November 8, 1960, p. 8.

44. *Ibid.,* November 7, 1960, sec. 3, p. 20.

45. *Ibid.,* November 8, 1960, p. 20.

46. *Supra,* p. 30.

47. See its June 26, 1960 editorial, quoted *supra,* pp. 25-26.

48. *Times-Picayune,* November 12, 1960, p. 10.

49. 

| | | |
|---|---|---|
| Kennedy | 407,515 | 50.4% of the total |
| Nixon | 231,193 | 28.6 |
| States' Rights | 169,861 | 21.0 |

Figures from Public Affairs Research Council of Louisiana, Inc., *PAR Analysis No. 91: Election Results, November* vtfj (Baton Rouge: December 1960), p. 2. In 1956, the state went for Eisenhower.

50. *Times-Picayune*, November 16, 1960, p. 2.
51. *Ibid.*, p. 19.
52. *Ibid.*
53. *Ibid.*, November 17, 1960, sec. 2, p. 11.
54. *Times-Picayune*, November 16, 1960, p. 31.
55. *Ibid.*, November 17, 1960, p. 6.
56. New Orleans Public Schools, *Facts and Finances*, 1959–1960, p. 39.
57. Report of the Louisiana State Advisory Committee to the United States Commission on Civil Rights, *The New Orleans School Crisis* (Washington: Government Printing Office, 1961), p. 23. Hereinafter referred to as Advisory Report.
58. Edward L. Pinney and Robert S. Friedman, *Political Leadership and the School Desegregation Crisis in Louisiana* (Eagleton Institute, "Cases in Practical Politics," Case 31; McGraw-Hill Book Company, 1963), p. 15. Hereinafter referred to as Pinney and Friedman.
59. *Southern School News*, December 1960, p. 10.
60. *Ibid.*, November 1960, p. 14.
61. *Bush v. Orleans Parish School Board; Williams v. Davis; U.S. v. State of Louisiana*, 188 F. Supp. 916 (1960). Declared unconstitutional in this decision were the following Acts of the first special session of 1960: Acts 2, 10, 11, 12, 13, 14, 16, 17, 18, 19, 20, 21, 22, 23, 24, 25, 26 and 27, and House Concurrent Resolutions 10 (placing an eight man legislative committee in control of the Orleans schools), 17 (transferring control of the Orleans schools to the legislature as a whole), 18 (firing Redmond and Rosenberg), 19 (declaring a school holiday for November 14), and 23 (removing from office the four school board members).
62. *Ibid.*, 364 U.S. 500 (1960).
63. This part of the story, centering on fiscal policy, is not fully germane to this discussion. For the interested reader, the story is documented in Pinney and Friedman and in *Southern School News*, January 1961, pp. 9 and 11, and February 1961, p. 6.
64. *Advisory Report*, p. 16.
65. *Ibid.*
66. *Times-Picayune*, December 9, 1960, p. 25.
67. *Southern School News*, January 1961, p. 10.
68. *Advisory Report, op. cit.*
69. *Wagner v. Redmond*, 127 So. 2nd 275 (February 20, 1961).
70. John Steinbeck, *Travels with Charley in Search of America* (New York: Bantam Books. 1963), pp. 255–56.
71. *Ibid.*, p. 257.
72. *New York Times*, December 5, 1960, p. 38.
73. Stan Opotowsky, "The News Mob," *Nation*, September 30, 1961, p. 203.
74. Daniel J. Boorstin, *The Image: A Guide to Pseudo-Events in America* (New York: Harper Colophon Books, 1964), p. 29.
75. Robert Coles, *Children of Crisis* (Boston: Little, Brown & Co., 1967) pp. 74–86.
76. Pinney and Friedman, p. 17.
77. Trillin, *New Yorker*, June 20, 1964, pp. 41–119.
78. *Supra*, p. 58.
79. *New York Times*, December 6, 1960, p. 1.

80. *Ibid.*, November 28, 1960, p. 1.
81. *Ibid.*
82. *Times-Picayune*, December 14, 1960, p. 12.
83. Wilma Dykeman and James Stokely, "Integration: Third and Critical Phase," *New York Times Magazine*, November 27, 1960, pp. 24–25.
84. *Times-Picayune*, January 31, 1961, p. 2.
85. *Ibid.*
86. *Ibid.*
87. *Ibid.*, November 5, 1960, sec. 3, p. 25.
88. *Time*, August 25, 1961, p. 40.
89. *Southern School News*, September 1961, p. 10.
90. *Ibid.*, p. 9.
91. *Ibid.*, October 1961, p. 2.
92. Ralph McGill, "The Crisis of the City," *Saturday Review*, May 23, 1959, p. 15.
93. Douglass Cater, "Atlanta: Smart Politics and Good Race Relations," *Reporter*, July 11, 1957, p. 18.
94. *Times-Picayune*, January 29, 1961, sec. 2, p. 2.
95. Warren Breed, *op. cit.*, p. 132.
96. Nelson W. Polsby, "The Sociology of Community Power: A Reassessment," *Social Forces*, XXXVII (March 1959), p. 233.
97. *Times-Picayune*, January 29, 1961, sec. 2, p. 4.
98. *Time*, August 17, 1962, p. 20.
99. *Southern School News*, November 1961, p. 8.
100. See V. O. Key, *Southern Politics in State and Nation* (New York: Vintage Books, 1949), pp. 164–179; Sindler, *Huey Long's Louisiana*; William C. Havard, Rudolf Heberle, and Perry H. Howard, *The Louisiana Elections of 1960* (Louisiana State University Studies, Social Science Series, no. 9; Baton Rouge: Louisiana State University Press, 1963).
101. E. L. Woodward, *The Age of Reform, 1815–1870* (Oxford: Oxford University Press, 1938), p. 34. I came across this quote in Morgenthau, *Scientific Man vs. Power Politics* (Chicago: University of Chicago Press, 1946), p. 124.

## Appendix I: SPECIAL SCHOOL BOARD SURVEY—MAY 9, 1960

|  | White Parents | Negro Parents | Totals |
|---|---|---|---|
| Number of votes to keep schools open | 2,820 (18.14%) | 12,017 (94.56%) | 14,837 |
| Number of votes to close schools | 12,724 (81.86%) | 691 ( 5.44%) | 13,415 |
| Number of votes counted | 15,544 | 12,708 | |
| Number of votes spoiled | 58 | 41 | |
| Total ballots returned | 15,602 | 12,749 | |
| Number of ballots mailed | 24,535 | 25,779 | |
| Return | 63.59% | 49.45% | |

## Appendix II: A DIGEST OF THE PRINCIPAL BILLS PASSED IN THE FIRST SPECIAL SESSION OF THE LOUISIANA LEGISLATURE, 1960

No. 1. Appropriated $168,000 to pay the costs of the session.

No. 2. Purported to interpose the sovereignty of the state between the federal government and the school board. Among many other things, this bill imposed criminal penalties upon anyone, including any officer of the federal government, who attempted to interfere with the state's control of education.

No. 10. Gave the governor power to close any school threatened by disorder or riots whenever in his judgment such acts may be anticipated.

No. 11. Gave the governor power to close any public school which "is under court order to carry out any program . . . not consistent with the constitution and laws of the state. . . ." Also gave the governor power to close any school where "the operation of such school . . . might cause friction or disorder. . . ." These powers to be given to the governor in his complete discretion.

No. 13. Withdrew state aid from any school operating either voluntarily or under court order contrary to the laws of the state.

No. 14. Ordered state supported colleges and universities not to recognize the graduation certificate of anyone coming from any school not being operated in accordance with the laws of the state.

No. 16. Removed restrictions on state police acting within municipalities maintaining their own police force.

No. 17. Withdrew all powers from the Orleans Parish school board and vested them in the legislature.

No. 18. Created a board of trustees to collect and administer the funds of any parish in which the school board has been abolished.

No. 20. Prohibited the state Board of Education from accrediting any school operating in violation of the laws of Louisiana.

No. 21. Prohibited school board members from performing any duty or function if his board has been ordered to carry out any program not consistent with the laws of the state. Violation of this provision would constitute grounds for removal from office.

No. 22. Required local school boards to close any school operated in violation of the laws of the state.

No. 23. Directed the state Board of Education to revoke the teacher's certificate of any teacher who teaches in a school not operating in accord with the laws of Louisiana.

No. 24. Provided that no pupil in a school operating in violation of the laws of the state shall be promoted or graduated.

No. 25. Repealed the Louisiana laws relating to the election and qualification of members of the Orleans Parish school board. This provision was to become effective immediately on passage and would render the November 8 election null. [The effect of this provision taken together with Bills 17 and 18 would have been to abolish the Orleans Parish school board.]

No. 26. Prohibited the transfer of pupils after the 21st day of the school year unless parents had moved. [School began on September 7.]

No. 27. Deleted from the law the requirement of compulsory attendance in private or public schools.

## Appendix III: ENDORSEMENT OF MATT SUTHERLAND

THE TIMES-PICAYUNE, NEW ORLEANS, LA., MONDAY MORNING, NOVEMBER 7, 1960

# "We believe that we and our children will all have a better future if

# MATT SUTHERLAND

### is re-elected to the

# SCHOOL BOARD"

This advertisement paid for by

| | | | |
|---|---|---|---|
| Darwin S. Fenner | Walter S. Simpson | J. E. Gould | Joseph McCloskey |
| Clifford F. Favrot | S. T. Alcus Jr. | William F. Grace | Edmund McIlhenny |
| Richard W. Freeman | Bruce K. Brown | Shirley B. Braselman | L. A. Merrigan |
| Louis Abramson Jr. | Edgar A. G. Bright | Donald H. Halsey | J. Reburn Monroe |
| James Henemann | William B. Monroe Sr. | W. S. Chadwick | Eben Hardie |
| George Montgomery | Russell Clark | Alfred Jay Moran | D. B. Cloudman |
| Sam Israel Jr. | E. V. Benjamin Jr. | James J. Coleman | Meyer Barton |
| John P. Labouisse | Joseph B. David Sr. | Ira R. Harkey | Louis B. Claverie |
| Gayle Dalferes | Robert T. Niesel, Ph.D. | Jerry K. Nicholson | Sumter D. Marks |
| Edward C. Norman, M.D. | Robert E. Craig II | Joseph M. Jones | Harry England |
| Nathaniel Curtis | Lester Kabacoff | Lyman L. Ellsey | Godfrey R. Parkerson |
| Ashton Phelps | Arthur O. Davis | Mark P. Lowrey | Paul Kapelow |
| George Pigman | Charles C. Deano | Samuel Karlin, M.D. | Paul O. H. Pigman |
| George Denegre | Harry B. Kelleher | Charles Keller Jr. | Donald W. Doyle |
| Malcolm Dinwiddie | Wallace C. Kemper | Nigel E. Rafferty | Herman S. Kohlmeyer Sr. |
| George B. Riviere | F. Monroe Labouisse | E. Harold Saer | James R. Lamantia Jr. |
| Frank Friedler Sr. | Shepard Latter | B. L. Layton | Earl R. LeCorgne Jr. |
| Stephen B. Lemann | Frank Strachan | G. Shelby Friedrichs | Roy M. Schwarz |
| Fisher Simmons | Howard J. Smith | R. Cornelius Smith | Charles G. Smither |
| James W. Smither Jr. | Maurice M. Stern | Percival Stern | Albert Terkuhle |
| Eli W. Tullis | Garner H. Tullis | Ernest C. Villere | Arthur J. Waechter Jr. |
| Robert M. Walmsley III | C. C. Walther | A. C. Waters Jr. | Arthur Waters |
| Paul T. Westervelt | H. Hunter White Jr. | George E. Williams Jr. | George G. Westfeldt Jr. |
| Laurence M. Williams | Albert J. Wolf | George Griswold | Paul McIlhenny |
| Rawley M. Penick Jr., M.D. | | | James M. Todd |

BUSINESS AND PROFESSIONAL MEN'S COMMITTEE FOR SUTHERLAND

## Appendix IV: THE APPEAL TO THE CITIZENS — DECEMBER 14, 1960

THE TIMES-PICAYUNE, NEW ORLEANS, LA., WEDNESDAY MORNING, DECEMBER 14, 1960          PAGE SEVEN—SECTION TWO

# We appeal to the citizens of New Orleans

**SEGREGATION OF RACES** in the schools of the South was first an absolute necessity and then a tradition. It is still our preference.

**SINCE THE 1954 DECISION** of the United States Supreme Court, and in the light of innumerable court decisions against the Orleans Parish School Board and other school authorities, it has been quite apparent to most of us that our system has become legally untenable and that some change must result.

**BECAUSE MANY CITIZENS** are convinced that these decisions are in violation of our nation's Constitution and Bill of Rights, it is well that this theory should be tested in the courts. The Louisiana Legislature has provided adequate basis for a proper test. Such tests within limits of discretion are proper and a part of our democratic privilege.

**BUT WE RECOGNIZE** that there is a price for a durable, workable democracy which citizens must pay in return for their freedoms. We believe that we are called upon to abide by the action of our legally constituted courts. If parts of our Constitution are found to be objectionable, then they may be amended in accordance with the law.

**WE BELIEVE** *that there should be an immediate end to threats, defamation and resistance to those who administer our laws. We appeal to the citizens of New Orleans to demand an end to the street demonstrations. We ask that support be given to the city officials, the police, and the duly elected School Board of the Parish of Orleans. We urge that education of our youth not be interrupted and that dignity be restored to our community.*

**WE ARE PROUD** we are citizens of the United States of America, and we recognize allegiance to this union. We ask others to join us in these sentiments.

Charles G. Smither
James J. Coleman
Frank A. M. Williams
W. B. Morroe
Ernest C. Villere
Albert J. Wall
Stanley E. Stumpf
Hughes Schneidau
A. L. Schlesinger Jr.
John L. C. Leslie
Clarence C. Clifton Jr.
Robert C. McIntyre
Robert Morse
Richard M. Page Jr.
F. G. Strachan
H. Grady Meador
F. Monroe Labouisse
Wood Brown
James W. Smither Jr.
C. A. Bartel
Gilbert M. Bisfeld

O. B. Cloudman
George R. Montgomery
Macy O. Teeter Jr.
Maurice J. Harton Jr.
Homer J. Dupuy, M.D.
Clifford A. King
Darwin S. Fenner
C. Alvin Bertel Jr.
Richard A. Stanley
Roger H. Doyle
Howard J. Smith
F. Harold Wirth D.D.S.
Buxton L. Layton Jr.
Robert T. Howard
Paul T. Westervelt
Sidney L. Ma-Is
William T. Hardie
Donald W. Doyle
Moise H. Goldstein
Herman S. Kohlmeyer
Frank Friedler

Eben Hardie
Peter H. Walmsley
G. Shelby Friedrichs
Martin A. Macdiarmid
George S. Farnsworth
Parks B. Pedrick
W. R. Arrowsmith, M.D.
Bruce K. Brown
Caswell P. Ellis III
Thomas N. Bernard
Roy O. Martin
Russell Clark
J. Herbert Williams
William P. Grace
Francis Dodd Menge
W. Ferguson Colcock
Maunsel W. Hickey
Gayle L. Dalferes
McDonald Stephens
J. Everett Eaves Sr.
John B. Smallpage

Barrett Kennedy, M.D.
Harry H. Hudson
W. Sherwood Collins
Pat F. Bass
Ralph M. Pons
William B. Dreux
E. N. Kearny Jr.
Harold V. Cummins, M.D.
Paul W. McIlhenny
Edward Matthews, M.D.
Brooke Duncan
Robert E. Wall
M. L. Michel, M.D.
John E. Hurley
Parks B. Pedrick Jr.
Herbert G. Johnske
Henry H. W. Ielles, M.D.
Edward A. McLellan
Donald H. Maloney
Richard C. Werner
E. James Koch

E. Stewart Maunsell
Abram H. Diaz, D.D.S.
Walter H. Weil Jr.
Paul D. Neil
H. R. Kehle, M.D.
I. William Ricciuti
W. W. Young Jr.
Moise W. Dennery
Frank B. Hayne
George T. Schneider, M.D.
Bruce Baird Jr.
Tom W. Avegno
M. E. Pohan
E. F. Creakmore
Charles A. Prachter
Robert A. Kottwitz Jr.
Alton Ochsner Jr., M.D.
Wallace C. Kamper
A. Miles Pratt
R. L. Atkinson Jr.
Jack C. Baumgartner

## BUSINESS AND PROFESSIONAL PEOPLE OF GREATER NEW ORLEANS

# Appendix V: A DECLARATION OF PRINCIPLES — AUGUST 31, 1961

THE TIMES-PICAYUNE, NEW ORLEANS, LA., THURSDAY MORNING, AUGUST 31, 1961     PAGE THIRTEEN—SECTION ONE

*Foreword:* Realizing that public education in Louisiana must be preserved; that law and order must be maintained in New Orleans; and the dignity of our city upheld before our countrymen and the world, citizens, whose names appear on this page have agreed upon a Declaration of Principles. We feel that every citizen can endorse this declaration. We feel that you stand with us in our determination to see t h a t *lawlessness, intimidation* and *coercion* are not tolerated in our city at any time, under any circumstances. We invite you to join us and support our stand. Simply write P. O. Box 881 to express *your desire* to help maintain the respect our city deserves.

*Committee for Louisiana*

# A
# DECLARATION
# of
# PRINCIPLES
## *Relative to our Urgent School Problem*

Public education in Louisiana must be preserved.

The people of each parish of the State, in accordance with the democratic concept of local self government, should be free to determine the basis on which their schools should be operated in compliance with the orders of the Federal Court.

Preservation of law and order in Louisiana requires compliance with the final decisions of the United States Supreme Court; any other course would result in chaos.

We believe that public education is reserved to the States and steps should be taken to enlist the aid and support of citizens throughout the nation with the view of eventual amendment of the Constitution of the United States in order to preserve the right of the States in education.

Although the private school system cannot become an adequate substitute for the public school system, and much less supplant it, the right of parents to send their children to private schools should be recognized.

The time has come for the reasonable men and women of Louisiana to express their views and to assume positions of leadership in this critical social problem in order that unity may be restored to our people.

Francis R. Abadie, DDS
Louis Abramson, Jr.
Nick J. Accardo, MD
Walter P. Adler
S. T. Aleus, Jr.
G. T. Alexander
Frank C. Allen
Albert L. Aschaffenburg
E. Lyle Aschaffenburg
Louis L. Babin
Roland Bahan
Bruce Baird, Jr.
James M. Baldwin
Stanley A. Baron, Sr.
Maurice F. Barr
Harry I. Barron
M. M. Bayon
Manley E. Beard
Robert H. Beattie
A. C. Bellande
Rabbi Leo A. Bergman
W. E. Bergman
Joseph Grima Bernard
Tom N. Bernard
Victor Bernard
C. Alvin Bertel, Jr.
Clement Betpouey, Jr.
Francis A. Bienvenu, Jr.
Douglas L. Black
G. M. Blefeld
W. A. Boudreaux, Sr.
Leslie Bowling
W. Hullin Bowman
J. J. Boyle
R. C. Brandt
P. M. Breckinridge
Frederic W. Brewer, MD
Edgar Bright, Jr.
Bruce X. Brown
Carl G. Buchmann
Morris W. Caldwell
A. G. Cambias, Jr.
Kermit Carr
Charles Cassing
Elmo J. Cerise, MD
W. S. Chadwick
John Chaffe
Harry N. Charbonnet
Larry Choppin
N. C. Church
Russell Clerk
Louis B. Claverie
Jamie Julian Coleman
James M. Colomb

James M. Colomb, Jr.
James Noone Connolly
Leo M. Coogan
Robert E. Craig, II
Robert H. Crane
Charles L. Crawford, Jr.
E. F. Creekmore
Gayle L. Dalferes
Arthur Q. Davis
Eugene Allen Davis
George Dawson
J. Maurice Dazet
Charles DeBlieux
Oliver Delery
Charles I. Denechaud, Jr.
George Denegre
C. S. DeWeese
Walter P. Dias, MD
Helion Dickson, Jr.
Donald W. Doyle
William B. Dreux
Brooke H. Duncan, Jr.
T. S. Dunn
Homer J. Dupuy, MD
Morgan G. Earnest
Elroy Eckhardt, Jr.
Caswell P. Ellis, III
Robert W. Elsasser
Mayo L. Emory, MD
Harry M. England
Joseph J. Falgout
Richard A. Faust, MD
Clifford F. Favrot
Gervais F. Favrot
Rabbi Julian B. Feibelman
Darwin S. Fenner
H. J. Ferry
Joseph Dorian Fleming, Jr.
Richard R. Foster
Gerland J. Foucha, Jr.
Richard W. Freeman
G. Shelby Friedrichs
M. G. Frey
Frank Friedler
Samuel Friedman
George S. Frierson, Jr.
O. L. Furse
Geo. C. Gahler
Edward W. Gaines
J. Garcia, MD
John Jim Garvey

Edwin Gaudet
Harold J. Geiger
Leon Godchaux, II
Paul V. Godfrey
Philip Ives Goodman
Kenneth Gormin
Robert E. Gough
William F. Grace
Algo I. Greenberg
Lee C. Grevemberg
Dr. J. D. Grey
Robert Guy
D. H. Halsey
C. Herbert Hamilton
Harry D. Hamilton
Eben Hardie
William T. Hardie
Ford Hardy
W. H. Harris, Jr., MD
Maurice Hartson, Jr.
L. A. Hattier
Frank B. Hayne
George W. Healy, Jr.
Isaac S. Heller
Lawrence H. Hennessey, Jr.
Jimmy Heymann
H. N. Hickey
Maumel W. Hickey
R. L. Hindermann
Alvin H. Howard
D. Douglas Howard
Killian Huger
John E. Hurley
James J. Impastato
Leon Irwin, Jr.
Sam Israel, Jr.
F. Jaubert, III
Pittman Johnson
Bishop Girault Jones
Joseph M. Jones
Thomas F. Jordan
P. W. Juge
Harry Gen. Gus Julian, O.M.I.
Richard B. Jurisich
Lester Kabacoff
Paul Kapelow
Murrel Kaplan, MD
Spencer L. Kearl
E. N. Kearny, Jr.
Donald E. Keenan
Harry R. Kelleher
Charles Keller, Jr.
James P. Kelly
W. C. Kemper
Clifford A. King

E. James Kock
Irvin J. Kohler
Robert Kottwitz, Jr.
F. Monroe Labouisse
John P. Labouisse
J. H. Lagarde
Lucius M. Lamar
O. Lambert
Charles W. Lane, III
Shepard M. Latter
Dell S. Lehon, DDS
Joseph E. Leininger
Thomas B. Lemann
Louis G. Lemle
Neville Levy
Fred E. Lind
S. H. Lochner
T. H. Lynch
William W. Martin
Harry McCall, Jr.
Richard McCarthy, Jr.
E. B. McCloskey
Richard B. McConnell
A. Q. Petersen
Edmund McIlhenny
Paul W. McIlhenny
Robert C. McIntyre
Edward A. McLellan
William C. McNeal
George F. Macdiarmid
Martin A. Macdiarmid
Walter S. Maestri, Jr.
Glen Magnuson
G. J. Marks, Jr.
Sidney L. Marks
Sumter D. Marks, Jr.
Rev. Harrison Martin
Paul A. Martin
Melvin W. Mathes
George B. Matthews
Clifton Meaux
F. D. Menga
John G. Menville, MD
L. A. Merrigan
M. L. Michel, MD
F. F. Michon
Henry H. W. Miles, MD
Michael J. Molony, Jr.
Joseph P. Monroe, Jr.
Malcolm L. Monroe
William B. Monroe
Charles N. Monsted

George R. Montgomery
Joseph W. Montgomery
D. W. Moore, DDS
Milton M. Moore
Alfred J. Moran
Robert Morss
W. U. Moss, Jr.
Robert T. Niesset
Paul D. Noll
George L. Nordhouse
B. F. Norman, Jr.
C. A. Norton
Alton Ochsner, MD
Alton Ochsner, Jr., MD
John L. Ochsner, MD
John R. O'Meallie
John M. O'Neill
James B. O'Rourke, Jr.
Neal Owens, MD
Richard M. Page
Peter E. Pattison
Parks B. Pedrick, Jr.
Parks B. Pedrick, Sr.
A. Q. Petersen
Ashton Phelps
Louis C. Philips
Shepard Pleasants
Edw. Poitevent
Ralph M. Pons
A. Miles Pratt
John J. Puissegur
Charles R. Ransom
A. Louis Read

A. G. Reese
Atwood L. Rice, Jr.
Dick Robbard, Jr.
Henry M. Robinson
James Roddy
Harold M. Rouchell
E. M. Rowley
John Y. Ruddock
William H. Saunders, Jr.
Maury L. Scheuermann
A. L. Schlesinger
Hughes Schneidau
Oscar Schneidau
James P. Schwart
Pohl Selley
John W. Sharp
Morgan L. Shaw
Thomas Sidney
J. W. Simon, Jr.
John W. Sims
Howard J. Smith
Robert Croft Smith, MD
Charles G. Smither
J. W. Smither, Jr.
Roy W. Speer
Joseph W. Stanley
Richard A. Stanley
Moise S. Steeg, Jr.
Edgar B. Stern, Jr.
Zachary A. Stern, Jr.
John O. Stuardi, Jr.
Geo. W. Sullivan
Macy O. Teetor, Jr.

R. Frank Thomas
John P. Tims
Canon William S. Turner
P. F. Vallon
Ernest C. Villere
Pierre Villere
A. J. Waechter, Jr.
Frank H. Walk
J. Mort Walker, Jr.
Peter H. Walmsley
R. M. Walmsley
John J. Weigel
Leo S. Weil
Calvin H. Weiser, Jr.
Jack M. Weiss
Seymour Weiss
Blaks West
George G. Westfeldt, Jr.
Harold Wheelahan
Morgan L. Whitney
John W. Whitty, Jr.
Urban C. Wilkinson
Dozier P. Willard
Frank A. M. Williams
Frank B. Williams
George E. Williams, Jr.
J. Calvin Williams
J. Herbert Williams
A. R. Wogan, Jr.
F. Harold Wirth, DDF
William B. Wisdom
Albert J. Wolf
Leon M. Wolf, Jr.
Harold W. Woods, Jr.
Brandon B. Woolley
W. W. Young, Jr.

## Appendix VI: SIGNERS AND CONTENT OF THE FOUR PUBLIC STATEMENTS

| Date | Subject | Number of signers | Number of top ten elite | Comment |
|------|---------|-------------------|-------------------------|---------|
| Nov. 7, 1960 | Support for Sutherland's reelection. | 98 | 6 | Made no mention of desegregation or of school board. |
| Nov. 17, 1960 | Deploring violence. | 160 | 7 | Praised mayor for preserving law and order; but made no mention of school board. This statement was issued at the request of the mayor and came the morning after riots and violence had erupted on the streets. |
| Dec. 14, 1960 | Deploring violence and calling for support of school board. | 105 | 1 | Boycott now one month old; Mardi Gras threatened. This was the first call for the support of the school board by an elite body. The one top elite on the ad was the single most influential elite. |
| Aug. 31, 1961 | Call for peaceful desegregation in compliance with orders of federal courts. | 315 | 9 | Before school opened the second year. |

# Index

# CENTER PUBLICATIONS

*The following material is available from the Center. Please note that publications must be ordered by number, and that payment must accompany the order.*

**THE CENTER FOR URBAN EDUCATION FACT SHEET.** A description of the history, current activities, and organization of the Center.

**THE CENTER FORUM,** a monthly newsletter that reports on the major issues facing schoolmen and parents in New York City and other urban areas. The coverage is topical and focuses on both the analysis of broad concepts and the description of current practices.

**THE URBAN REVIEW,** is published bimonthly during the school year. Its purpose is to stimulate discussion problems and potentialities of education in the urban environment. This purpose is in keeping with the fundamental objective of the Center, which is to contribute strategic knowledge and resources toward improving the quality of teaching and learning in urban society.

**SCHOOL INTEGRATION. A COMPREHENSIVE CLASSIFIED BIBLIOGRAPHY OF 3100 REFERENCES edited by Meyer Weinberg.** Copies avail-available at $2.00 each  ■  C001

This exhaustive compilation includes numerous unpublished and fugitive materials. The entries are arranged into 16 sections, with brief introductions to each section. A complete author index is also included.

**URBAN EDUCATION BIBLIOGRAPHY compiled and annotated by Helen Randolph.** Single copies on request. Additional copies $1.00 each  ■  B005

This bibliography, covering the period from September 1964 through December 1965, annotates and classifies over a thousand items, and includes an additional four hundred unannotated items drawn from the same period.

## PUBLIC RECREATION AND THE NEGRO. A STUDY OF PARTICIPA-TION AND ADMINISTRATIVE PRACTICES by Richard Kraus. Single copies on request. Additional copies as follows: 1—20, 25¢ each; 21—50, 20¢ each; over 50, 15¢ each ■ B001

Professor Kraus has interviewed recreation directors and administrators of schools and parks in the five boroughs of New York City and in 24 suburban communities in New York, New Jersey, and Connecticut, and from these interviews has drawn a portrait of Negro participation in public recreation. His study indicates that the interests and needs of Negroes are not being adequately met. Professor Kraus' findings are relevant to the broad problem of alleviating racial tensions by improving the character of community life .

## LEARNING READINESS IN TWO JEWISH GROUPS. A STUDY IN "CUL-TURAL DEPRIVATION" by Morris Gross, with an introduction by John Seeley. Single copies on request. Additional copies as above ■ B003

Comparing two groups of middle class, American-born, Jewish, preschool children, Dr. Gross finds differences in their learning readiness that compare to the sorts of differences found in studies that juxtapose the relative advantages of middle class white children against those of poor Negro children. Dr. Gross, in other words, has found a case of "educational disadvantage" among children from middle class Jewish families, and so throws open the whole question of what "disadvantage" means and what its causes are likely to be. Dr. Gross asks: how are we to understand "educational disadvantage" if it does not have an economic base?

## THE NEGRO IN SCHOOLROOM LITERATURE by Minnie W. Koblitz. Single copies on request. Additional copies as above. Third printing ■ B002

An annotated bibliography of classroom reading materials that portray integrated situations. The biliography is designed especially for use by elementary school teachers and librarians, and focuses on material for kindergarten through the sixth grade. Current through September 1966.

## THE SCHOOL IN THE MIDDLE: DIVIDED OPINION ON DIVIDING SCHOOLS edited by Lawrence J. Barnett, Gerald Handel, and Helen Weser. Single copies on request. Additional copies $1.00 each ■ B007

The middle school versus the junior high school is the subject of this collection of 30 recent articles and speeches by educators. Their views cover the spectrum of current theory and practice of representative school systems across the country. The anthology incorporates general considerations of the design, objectives, and status of the middle school, as well as a detailed study of the New York City middle-school program.

## GREATER NEW YORK ART DIRECTORY edited by Thomas J. Scott.
Single copies on request. Additional copies $1.00 each  ■  **B009**

This is a reference guide to the art resources available in the region to teachers and students. Schools, museums and libraries, galleries, publications, and community organizations are arranged in alphabetical order and by location in the metropolitan New York area. Personnel connected with art education are listed in separate sections. An index is included.

---

*The following material has been published for the Center by Frederick A. Praeger, Inc., and is available from bookstores or directly from the publishers (111 Fourth Avenue, New York, N.Y. 10003).*

## THE URBAN R's edited by Robert A. Dentler, Bernard Mackler, and Mary Ellen Warshauer. Clothbound, $7.50. Paperbound, $2.50  ■  **C002 Cloth, C003 Paper**

A collection of 18 articles—16 published for the first time—that focuses on the general question of how the school, together with the community, can provide a meaningful education for the changing population of the children in our urban centers.

## BIG CITY DROPOUTS AND ILLITERATES by Robert A. Dentler and Mary Ellen Warshauer. Revised edition. Clothbound, $10.00  ■  **C013**

This study examines the social and economic correlates of high school withdrawal and adult functional illiteracy. The study is based on a multiple regression analysis that draws on data from 131 large cities throughout the United States. The authors give special attention to the instances where the rates of withdrawal and illiteracy are higher than expected. In their conclusion, they discuss the implications of their findings for federal, state, and local programs designed to combat the problems they have examined.

## PARTICIPANTS AND PARTICIPATION: A STUDY OF SCHOOL POLICY IN NEW YORK CITY by Marilyn Gittell. Clothbound, $7.50. Second printing  ■  **C004**

This study examines how the New York City school system makes its decisions. It focuses particularly on the question of how much influence the community at large has in the process. Against a detailed description of the school administration, Dr. Gittell examines five policy areas: budget, curriculum, choosing a superintendent, salaries, and integration.

The following films are available from Association Films, Inc., 600 Grand Ave., Ridgefield, New Jersey 07657.

**"NO LITTLE HOPE,"** a 28-minute color 16mm sound film, which reflects through the voices and ideas of parents in New York City the Center's own broad notion of urban education—the problems, the possibilities. Available for sale $200 a copy.

**"GREEN YEARS,"** a 28-minute color 16mm film, which shows how education takes place in an informal instructional way in the city's parks. Available for sale $200 a copy.

A list of Center reports and evaluations is available upon request. These studies contain the findings of the Center's research and development activity. ■ **A101**

☆GPO 961-236